Tax Guide 405

SELLING
YOUR
BUSINESS

by

Holmes F. Crouch
Tax Specialist

Published by

Allyear Tax Guides

20484 Glen Brae Drive
Saratoga, CA 95070

ISBN 0-944817-56-4

LCCN 98-70251

Printed in U.S.A.

Series 400
Owners and Sellers

Tax Guide 405

SELLING YOUR BUSINESS

For other titles in print, see page 224.

The author: **Holmes F. Crouch**
For more about the author, see page 221.

PREFACE

If you are a knowledge-seeking **taxpayer** looking for information, this book can be helpful to you. It is designed to be read — from cover to cover — in less than eight hours. Or, it can be "skim-read" in about 30 minutes.

Either way, you are treated to **tax knowledge** . . . *beyond the ordinary*. The "beyond" is that which cannot be found in IRS publications, FedWorld on-line services, tax software programs, or on CD-ROMs.

Taxpayers have different levels of interest in a selected subject. For this reason, this book starts with introductory fundamentals and progresses onward. You can verify the progression by chapter and section in the table of contents. In the text, "applicable law" is quoted in pertinent part. Key phrases and key tax forms are emphasized. Real-life examples are given . . . in down-to-earth style.

This book has 12 chapters. This number provides depth without cross-subject rambling. Each chapter starts with a head summary of meaningful information.

To aid in your skim-reading, informative diagrams and tables are placed strategically throughout the text. By leafing through page by page, reading the summaries and section headings, and glancing at the diagrams and tables, you can get a good handle on the matters covered.

Effort has been made to update and incorporate all of the latest tax law changes that are *significant* to the title subject. However, "beyond the ordinary" does not encompass every conceivable variant of fact and law that might give rise to protracted dispute and litigation. Consequently, if a particular statement or paragraph is crucial to your own specific case, you are urged to seek professional counseling. Otherwise, the information presented is general and is designed for a broad range of reader interests.

The Author

INTRODUCTION

Selling your **business** is a much different process from that of selling your auto or home. You are selling multiple assets — tangible and intangible — each of which has to be independently valued on its own. When you sell them as a "bundle" instead of independently, you add a third dimension called: **goodwill** or, **going concern value**. In some cases, the value of goodwill can exceed that of any other single asset of the sale. But, it cannot be sold alone. You must sell the entire business in packaged form.

Pricing your business for sale becomes a real challenge. This is because there are few comparable sales that you can use as a guide. Chances are, you are selling one of a kind. This necessitates — at the very minimum — **three** different pricing and appraisal techniques. From these, you choose a "weighted average." We'll tell you of nine different methods you can use, and of the special rules for valuing goodwill and other intangibles.

Necessarily, we must limit the scope and focus of this book. When we address "Selling YOUR Business," we are referring to a small business. How big is "small"? Answer: Under $10,000,000 (10 million) in total assets and having 35 or fewer co-owners.

Why do we pick the number of 35 owners or less? Answer: Because there are favorable tax rules that apply to small business corporations — whether "C" or "S" types — and because of certain exemptions from the securities laws for restricted/unregistered stock. Otherwise, the form of business may be a proprietorship, partnership, or corporation — it doesn't matter.

When selling any business, there are tax consequences to pay. There is no way around these consequences. Even so-called "tax-free exchanges" that you may have heard about, are not tax free. If stringent like-class conditions are met, portions of the sale may be tax deferred. Obviously, the challenge is to minimize the total tax bite as legitimately as you can. This can be done by structuring the sale to take advantage of the treatment accorded to capital gains and to ordinary losses. We have numerous pointers for you in this regard . . . if you do your homework.

Federal law requires that the IRS (Internal Revenue Service) be notified when you sell your business. Under the mandate of IR Code Section 6045: *Information Returns of Brokers*, the title company (or other agent) closing the sale must report the GROSS PROCEEDS of the sale. In addition, state laws require that a

Notice of Bulk Sale be published periodically in a newspaper of general circulation in the area where you do business. The net result is that the moment your sale closes, you are under continuous COMPUTER SURVEILLANCE . . . by all tax, legal, and regulatory agencies. We address these matters herein.

For any gross sale price, there is an ongoing tax-bone of contention between buyer and seller. The contentious issue is the valuation of goodwill and its associated intangibles: covenant not to compete, customer lists, operational know-how, etc. For years, the IRS held intransigently that goodwill, etc. was a capital asset. This meant that the seller got capital gain treatment, whereas the buyer had his money tied up indefinitely — no amortization writeoffs of any kind. Upon acquisition, a capital asset had "indeterminable life," the IRS asserted. In one notable case (*Newark Morning Ledger Co. v. U.S., S Ct, 93-1 USTC ¶ 50,228*), the IRS had tied up $67,773,000 (nearly 68 million) this way.

On April 20, 1993 the IRS lost its stand in the U.S. Supreme Court. Subsequently, Congress came to its senses and enacted IRC Section 197: *Amortization of Goodwill and Certain Other Inangibles*. Goodwill, etc. can now be amortized over 15 years . . . instead of none at all. We'll tell you about this exciting new development in Chapter 4.

Whether selling a proprietorship, partnership, or corporation, there are two unusual tax forms that you need to know about. One is **Form 4797**: *Sales of Business Property*; the other is **Form 8594**: *Asset Acquisition Statement*. We devote a separate chapter to each of these forms. In the everyday course of your business operations, the two forms are not involved. But when your business is sold, they become VERY important.

Why so?

Because Forms 4797 and 8594 are the only way that you can combat the IRS's incessant surveillance demands for 100% tax — plus penalties and interest — on the gross sale amount (*without any deductions or offsets*). Each of these forms (and only these forms) has a single entry box for direct matching that which is stuck in the IRS's computer craw. Ignore these forms at your peril.

We cover other forms; we cite applicable tax law provisions; and we give practical pointers and suggestions throughout this book. We do all of this because, in a complex transaction such as the sale of a business, we want you to do things right!

CONTENTS

1

PREPARATORY MATTERS

A Solvent Business With "Going Concern Value" (Called: MOMENTUM Or Goodwill) Comprises The Best Potential For Sale. Even So, Much Preparatory Effort Is Required To Induce A Prospective Buyer. The Entire "Bundle Of Assets" Must Be Identified With Specificity And All Ownership Interests Must Be Clarified. Such Matters As History Of The Business, Reasons For Selling, Current Net Worth, And Three Years Of Tax Returns Are Very Important. Of These Items, Your Tax Returns Are An Indicator Of How Well You Run Your Business, And Are Regarded As Prima Facie Verification Of The Facts And Figures You Cite To A Potential Buyer.

Selling a business — a *small* business, particularly — is unlike selling shares in a mutual fund, or stocks through a broker. Nor is it like selling your personal residence. Nor like selling your golf clubs or ski equipment. Nor like selling your old car. If there is any functional analogy here at all, selling a business is like selling all of these items together . . . in one bulk transaction. You don't sell a solvent business one asset at a time.

There are two fundamental differences between selling a business and selling personal assets. These differences exist whether the business is personally owned by one individual, by an individual and his spouse, or by two or more co-owners. The two differences are: (1) *going concern value*, and (2) *allocation consistency* (between seller and buyer).

When a business is sold, the buyer (in most cases) wants to continue the business in one form or another. Because of this, he expects that your business has some "going concern value" to him. This is also called: *goodwill*. The buyer wants your customer goodwill and going concern value to carry him for a time, without too great an effort on his part. For this, he is willing to pay an amount over and above the pricing value of all tangible and intangible assets of the business that he buys.

Once the value of your business goodwill is established, and the sale closes, there follow very stringent tax allocation consistency rules for you and the buyer. Getting ready for these matters is what this chapter is all about. You don't sell a business on the spur of the moment. There is a lot of background information you need, and a lot of preparatory homework to do.

Our premise here and throughout this book is that you are facing the first sale of your business. Or, it could be the second sale of your business, having made mistakes in the first sale that you do not want to repeat. This time you want to do things right by getting prepared more methodically.

What Is a "Business"?

If you are thinking of selling your business, you first need to know if it is indeed a "business" that you are selling. What you may think of as a business, may not be so. If you sell a business, certain tax rules apply; if you sell a nonbusiness, different tax rules apply. Whatever you sell in this day and age is reported to Big Brother: the Internal Revenue Service (IRS). It is the gross sale price that is reported. Unless you can establish that it was a business that you sold, you could wind up paying income tax on the sale price alone . . . without any offsets. It behooves you, therefore, to know whether what you are selling is a tax qualified business.

The federal tax code (namely: Internal Revenue Code) characterizes all commercial businesses under the generic term: *trade or business*. This is construed to mean a trade, business, or profession in which the owner thereof is carrying on the activity for livelihood purposes or certainly for profit. Furthermore, the activity must be one through which a product or service, or combination, is offered to the general public at large. The offering must be on a continuing and ongoing basis, and not be intermittent. At all times, a profit motive must be present and some type of economic transaction between unrelated parties must be conducted.

For purposes of showing a profit motive, an activity is not a business if it is entered into for self-fulfillment, philosophical engagement, pursuing one's own investments, has the characteristics of a hobby, or is an occasional sale of some item produced or refurbished by the taxpayer. Those who pursue an activity full time, in good faith, with regularity, and with the expectation of producing income — more or less regularly — are said to be in a trade or business. The defining characteristic of such an activity is that it tends to take on a "momentum of its own."

What keeps the momentum going?

It is that unique combination of financial resources, materials and supplies, machinery and equipment, real estate and structures, labor and workmanship, technical and professional expertise, advertising and sales effort, customer service, and — yes — that always present element of market risks. Once a business is up to its cruising speed (so to speak), it tends to feed on and regenerate itself. The result is that repetitive business transactions often take place without much direct attention on the owner's part.

It is this momentum-for-profit that truly separates a business from nonbusiness activities. In a nonbusiness, the moment the owner stops his attention, the activity ceases. In contrast, in a business, the activity keeps rolling along. This momentum factor alone is what potential buyers are most interested in. Otherwise, the assets of what is perceived to be a business can be sold one at a time, rather than in bulk.

We present in Figure 1.1 an overview of what constitutes a potential business for sale. The essence is that you have to have a viable activity that will practically "sell itself."

Identify Your Asset Bundle

Once you are convinced that you have a tax qualified business to sell, there is preparatory step No. 1 to take. This step requires that you identify with specificity the assets that comprise your business. That is, if you are aware that a business is a *bundle* of assets, what is the specific bundle or "package" you are going to offer? In the identification process, keep the primary interest of the buyer in mind. He wants a package that will keep going on its own for awhile. Therefore, you want to identify your assets in a manner that projects your business to be as self-sufficient as possible.

To illustrate what we mean, consider three different businesses, namely: (1) an electrical contractor, (2) a retail clothing shop, and

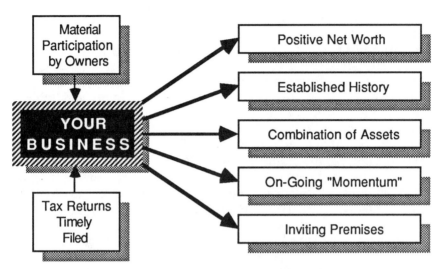

Fig. 1.1 - Desirable Features in a Prospective Business for Sale

(3) a dental office. Each has been in business more than five years; each has been modestly successful; each is being offered for sale for valid reasons. What are the assets that each has that a potential buyer would want?

In the case of the electrical contractor, he would likely have one or more vans and trucks fitted out for hauling materials, supplies, and tools to various worksites. For distant worksites, he has a clean and well-stocked small house trailer for living away from home up to five days at a time. He has close contacts with several reputable general contractors who engage his services statewide. He has some very special tools and equipment which enable him to do a job efficiently and expeditiously. He has his own customer base in the metropolitan area where he resides. And, of course, he has a telephone answering service and a paging system, but no prospective buyer would likely want these.

In the case of the clothing shop, there is an inventory of quality merchandise that any prospective buyer would surely want. It has already been ordered, stocked, and priced. The shop owner has a long-term lease in a commercial building to which he has made various leasehold improvements. He also has clothing racks, display counters, try-on rooms, signs and posters, cash registers, bar code scanners, office equipment, security systems, and so on. The shop is located in a magnet-type shopping mall, with plenty of parking space, security-patrolled 24 hours a day. The shop owner has a substantial repeat-customer base and has long-term relationships with established clothing suppliers.

In the case of the dental office, the dentist is a part owner in the professional building where his office is located. He has the latest technology of dental chairs, hygienist chairs, X-ray equipment, dark room, dental lab, sterilization equipment, supply room, toilet facilities, waiting room furnishings, window decorations, etc. He has a computer tracking and billing system for well over 1,000 patients who visit his office at least once a year or more. As a general practitioner, he has developed a referral network of dental specialists, such as orthodontists, endodontists, implant specialists, oral surgeons, and the like. This business owner is approaching the point of retirement.

All that we are trying to display in the three examples above is that different businesses have different assets to sell. That is, each business has its own "momentum bundle." It is up to each business owner, therefore, to dissect his business asset by asset, and lay it out in an orderly fashion . . . **on paper.** Every prospective buyer, at some point in the overview of your business, wants to see your asset listing. We are going to tell you much more about this asset-listing process in the next chapter. In the meantime, who is the owner of the business that is being offered for sale?

Clarify Ownership Interests

You cannot sell something (legally) which you do not own. No buyer is going to be interested in a business unless he can be satisfied that he will have clear title to it after the sale. This means that the owner or owners of a for-sale business must review all of the asset holdings and clarify any ownership discrepancies and contentions that may exist. This is preparatory step No. 2. For businesses that have been in operation 5, 10, 15, or more years, ownership matters tend to collect dust in the woodwork of memory and time.

If only one person — man or woman — has been 100% owner of the business from "day 1," there are usually no title transfer problems at time of sale. There may be asset allocation and pricing problems, but no conflict-of-ownership problems.

But, suppose there is a husband-and-wife business. Which one owns it? Unless they are formal business partners (as well as being marriage partners), only one spouse can be the sole proprietor. The proper one is he/she who is the primary provider of expertise and service that makes the business go. If there is controversy on this point, there can be transfer problems at time of sale.

There WILL BE transfer problems should the spouses be contemplating divorce — or be in the throes of it — at time of sale. No prospective buyer wants to become involved in interspousal ownership claims and counter-claims. If divorce is indeed imminent, get the marriage dissolved first. In so doing, property settlement and business ownership issues can be resolved under court supervision. Thereafter, the allocation of the business by the court to one or both spouses is treated as legal evidence of its ownership at time of sale.

Similarly, for husband-and-wife businesses which have been transferred into a family trust for estate planning purposes. In this case, the business is in the trust's name: not that of the husband nor that of the wife. If the arrangement is a revocable living trust, the business should be withdrawn from the trust and retitled in the name of either the husband or the wife. If the business is in an irrevocable living trust, particularly if one of the tax-exempt charitable-remainder types, the trustee is the person with whom the buyer has to deal. If the trustee happens to be the husband or the wife, and either or both are trustors (transferors/grantors) and beneficiaries of the trust, tax and legal invalidation rules come into play. Our thesis is that any business which is in an irrevocable living trust would be unsalable until at least one of the trust creators dies. And, even then, the retitling and legal entanglements would dissuade all but the shrewdest bargain-hunting buyers.

In intrafamily businesses (two brothers, brother and sister, two sisters, father and son, mother and daughter, and so on), there are ownership clarification problems also. Usually, these businesses are a word-of-mouth partnership, with no formal written agreement. If such is the case, the preparatory step for sale is to have a partnership, joint venture, or other co-ownership agreement drawn up. Then specify clearly therein the agreed ownership percentage of each participant. Prepare a formal document to this effect and have it notarized.

In the case of co-ownership of real estate which is part of the business being offered for sale, the recorded title to the property needs to be exhumed and examined. Chances are that, for ownerships other than between husbands and wives, the title would be in tenants-in-common form. If so, and if the percentage of ownership of each party is not clearly specified, an owner's conference must be called to sort these matters out. Thereupon, the recorded title should be amended to spell out each owner's interest, such as—

Owner A:	0.4056	(or 40.56%)
Owner B:	0.3489	(or 34.89%)
Owner C:	0.2455	(or 24.55%)
	1.0000	(or 100%)

If the business for sale is in corporate form and closely-held (five or fewer persons owning 51% or more of the business), chances are the ownership interests would be spelled out in the articles of incorporation, as amended. If not, the current shareholder registry has to be examined. From this registry of each person's shareholdings in the business, each principal's share has to be computed and verified. A formal entry would then have to be made in the minutes of a special shareholder's meeting to "officialize" each owner's just-before-sale ownership interest.

There is a point to all of the above. If there are two or more owners of a business, there is no point in offering the business for sale until each owner's interest is specifically clarified. This needs to be done to the "fourth decimal place." Nothing is more chilling to a prospective buyer than being drawn into a squabble between multiple co-owners.

Prepare History of Business

Once the ownership issues have been clarified, the next preparation-for-sale step (No. 3) is to review and record the history of your business. Go back to the days when it was first started. Dig up old records, photographs, and advertisements therewith. Recount how the business idea was formulated. Spell out what customer need it then fulfilled, and how those customer needs have changed and grown over the years. Outline all of the trials and tribulations of those early years and — if you can do so — describe that divine spark or lucky break that really got your business going. In other words, prepare a *business plan in reverse*, as it were.

Your objective is to prepare a 5- to 25-page pamphlet that covers all phases of the business from startup to its offer for sale. Use your existing staff and equipment for this purpose. If such is inadequate, engage a free-lance business historian or technical writer to assist in the effort. Make enough copies to have available for each prospective buyer, each sales broker who actively participates, each business owner (as a memoir), and each employee past and present. Where possible, mention the duties, devotions, and accomplishments of each long-term employee who is onboard at time of sale. This is important for employee resumé purposes should the new owner wish to change employees or bring in new hires of his own.

For prospective buyers, the main purpose of the history is to acquaint them with the evolution of the products and services of the business. Which product lines succeeded; which failed. Which services succeeded, and which failed. What made for the successes; what lessons were learned from the failures. What was the role of government and its regulations in the successes and failures. What kind of equipment and environment worked best. What particular technology advances had the greatest beneficial impact on the business. How did the local economy — and the national economy — change over the years, and what influences did these changes have on the business.

Devote a separate section to your current product line and services. List the names, addresses, phone numbers, and key persons of your suppliers, maintenance contractors, outside vendors, consultants, and other services that you have engaged from time to time.

Devote a separate section also to your customer base. Describe the type of customers that you have and have had, and why (if you know) they have ceased doing business with you over the years. List your current repeat customers and the approximate dollar amount of business that each does with you each year.

A prospective buyer would want this kind of information and more, as a guide to his assessment of the ongoing potential of your business. Furthermore, if accurately documented, the compilation itself becomes an asset of the business . . . with its own price tag at time of sale.

Good Reasons for Selling

Preparation-for-sale step No. 4 is to know your reason for selling, and stand by it. Don't try to be too clever in concealing whatever the real reason may be. If you are on the verge of bankruptcy, or are a defendant in major litigation which may drive you into bankruptcy, you should think twice before offering your business for sale. You've got to have a better reason for selling than simply trying to avoid bankruptcy.

Likewise, if your state of mind and insolvency are such that abandonment or foreclosure by creditors is an option, don't try to deceive a prospective buyer. It is better to sell whatever assets you can, one at a time, or put them on the block in a fire sale or a public auction.

But, if your business is sound and modestly successful, offering it for sale as a going concern is more satisfying. That is, provided you have a bona fide reason for the sale.

There is no law requiring that you have a reason for selling. As the owner or part-owner, you can sell whatever and whenever you want to. Yet, every prospective buyer is going to inquire why you are doing so. He may not really care. But he wants to be satisfied that you are not hiding something that he is bound to find out later. Otherwise, you may have a post-sale lawsuit for fraud or misrepresentation on your hands.

Owners sell their businesses for many reasons. The one reason you particularly want to avoid is transferring to an unsuspecting buyer your unresolved tax and legal problems. Among the more common bona fide reasons for selling a business are:

1. The owner wants to retire. If there are two or more co-owners, the senior owner may want to retire and talks the others into going along.

2. Serious illness or injury to an owner, or to a close member of his family.

3. Desire to move on to other bigger and better business ventures; needs money for the new startup.

4. Just plain tired of the frustrations and stresses of the business, from which the owner needs a long-term rest.

5. Technology advances have overtaken the owner, who does not have the financial resources or inclinations to modernize his activities.

6. Sudden growth in business requiring more expertise and market outlets than the current owner has access to.

7. One co-owner has an urgent personal need for money; another co-owner buys him out, then offers the business for sale.

8. Bickering among co-owners and their spouses; accusations of embezzlement of funds and misuse of business property. The only resolution is to sell the business.

9. Owners become lethargic; they are more interested in their personal enjoyment of life than in "minding the store."

10. Irritations and disgust with repetitive government agency audits, mandates, regulations, and penalties; owner spending more time defending himself against those "harassing partners" than in serving his customers.

As long as one's reasons for selling are sincere, valid, and believable, there are usually no adverse consequences to the buyer. As long as the business has ongoing momentum value, a prospective buyer may see a challenge which he cherishes. And thus, eventually, the business will sell.

Clear Out Your Junk

Preparation-for-sale step No. 5 is to clean up the business premises, fresh paint it if you will, and clear out all of your junk. Don't put it in a junk pile for visiting prospective buyers to see. Have it hauled away. If it has any salvage value to second-hand users, sell it or give it to established salvage dealers. If it has any value to charitable or educational institutions, give it to them.

Our point is: Get rid of your junk and unusable items any way you can. Don't try to foist it off on a prospective buyer. He is more interested in the challenges ahead than he is in rummaging through the junk and obsolescence of your business past.

For some mysterious reason, many business owners keep on hand old vehicles, machinery, equipment, damaged merchandise, unsalable inventory, obsolete stationery and supplies, long-ago paid-off accounts, and other miscellaneous in-the-way collectibles. Yes, some day an owner may be able to re-use it. But a prospective buyer isn't the least bit interested in said junk. In fact, to an astute buyer, the sight of junk in various corners and storage areas of the business-for-sale premises tells him that "something is wrong" with the owner. Possibly the owner is lazy, poorly self-disciplined, or is someone who can't make clean-cut decisions. The buyer may sense that he may have problems with the owner, should his interest approach the closing stages of a sale. Any experienced broker will tell you that junk lying around your business premises will severely dampen most prospects for a sale.

If you are going to sell your business, you might as well clean it up and get going.

Get Tax Returns in Order

Preparatory step No. 6 is to get all of your tax returns in order. Do this for the most recent three years of filings. You don't need more than three years of returns for the buyer, unless you have prior-year matters which are still pending. If you do have any unresolved tax matters, try to get them resolved — without arbitrarily conceding them — before the first serious potential buyer comes along.

When we say "all" tax returns, we mean the following (as applicable):

1. Income tax returns (federal and state)
2. Employee tax returns (quarterlies)
3. Nonemployee information returns
4. Sales and use tax returns (state)
5. Federal excise tax returns
6. Local property tax returns

If you have any outstanding tax deficiencies, liens, levies, or seizure notices, these too should be gathered up.

You have filed all of your required returns, haven't you? If so, gather them and organize them for each type of return. Don't disrupt your regular filing system for this. Instead, make photocopies and arrange each three years of return-types into a bound pamphlet of its own. Putting tax papers loosely in a folder, to be shown to a prospective buyer, will only cause mixups and misunderstandings. A separate pamphlet for each return-type can be presented and retrieved readily.

Why go through all of this effort? There are three reasons actually:

One. Keeping up to date on all tax matters is, perhaps, the best indicator of how well you run your business. Yes, we know: all taxes are a perennial irritant. Falling behind in tax filings and payments only puts you on that endless treadmill of trying to catch up. So, get caught up now.

Two. Any prospective buyer wants to be satisfied that, if he buys your business, he will not be stuck with your tax problems. Tax agencies are nasty and vindictive. They habitually go after the most recent "possessor of property" when they issue liens, levies, and seizure notices. If a new owner is going to be harassed for your delinquencies, you will have a post-sale lawsuit on your hands.

Three. Tax return information is treated as prima facie verification of facts and figures regarding your business. You have signed these returns *under penalties of perjury*. This signaturization alone gives your returns more credence than any oral statements you make.

If, within the recent past, any tax return has been audited, have that audit file separately packaged and available. If an audit has been started, but is not completed, have that file available also. Any new buyer will be interested in knowing what audit issues were raised, and what the outcome was . . . or is likely to be. A recent tax audit of your business implies that the new owner may get a *period of grace* before he, too, has to suffer the same ordeal.

Update Your Balance Sheet

Preparatory step No. 7 is to review your assets and liabilities, as reflected on your tax returns, then update your balance sheet. If your total assets exceed your total liabilities, you have a positive net worth. This means that you are solvent. The fact that you are solvent is what a potential buyer wants to see early on. The magnitude of your net worth — whether it is $100,000 or $1,000,000 or $10,000,000 — is not too important at this step. But you have to have some figures to show right up front.

If you file a proprietorship return, Schedule C or Schedule F (Form 1040), there is no balance sheet on the return. This means that you have to prepare one on your own. To assist you in this regard, Figure 1.2 is a good starting outline.

SMALL BUSINESS BALANCE SHEET		Prior Ending	Current Ending
Assets			
1	Cash on hand		
2	Accounts receivable		
3	Inventory on hand		
4	Loans & notes (TO others)		
5	Other current assets		
6	Land (net of improvements)		
7	Depreciable assets		
	● Less accumulated depreciation		
8	Intangible assets		
	● Less accumulated amortization		
9	All other assets (itemize)		
	Total Assets ➔		
Liabilities			
10	Accounts payable		
11	Loans payable		
12	Notes payable (less than 1 year)		
13	Other current liabilities		
14	Notes payable (1 year or more)		
15	All other liabilities (itemize)		
	Total Liabilities ➔		
	NET WORTH ▶▶ Total Assets Minus Total Liabilities		

Fig. 1.2 - Generalized Balance Sheet for Establishing Net Worth

If you file a partnership tax return (Form 1065), there is a balance sheet thereon. It is designated as Schedule L: *Assets, Liabilities and Capital.* If you file a corporate return (Forms 1120 for "C" type or 1120S for "S" type), its balance sheet is also

Schedule L: *Assets, Liabilities and Shareholder's Equity*.
The information you already have on these balance sheets comprises
the starting point for your updating effort.

The balance sheets on your partnership or corporate returns are
posted to the end of your taxable year. Often, this is not done until
several months or more following the end of your tax year. This
means that they are more than 30 days out of date. The updating
challenge, therefore, is to keep your balance sheet information to
within 30 days of the preceding ending month.

Figure 1.2 is a composite of the balance sheet information found
on partnership and corporate tax returns. It is generalized enough to
be useful to any small business. When summarized on a single
sheet of paper, and presented to a prospective buyer, he can get an
instant handle on what your principal assets are . . . and your
principal liabilities. This can be the start of an in-depth discussion
on where and how your business can be improved and expanded.

The net worth from your balance sheet constitutes the *book
value* of your business. This is **not** the market value or the price for
which you would be willing to sell. It simply reflects your tax
accounting methods and procedures through the years. The book
value of a solvent business is always lower than its fair market
value.

For example, you bought a piece of equipment for the business
several years ago. Your initial cost was $50,000 (say). Because of
the particular way you depreciated it for tax purposes, its current
undepreciated value on your books is $10,000. Yet, if you were to
buy the same equipment in the second-hand market it would cost
you $25,000. Thus, your book value of $10,000 has no correlation
to the market value of $25,000.

Market valuing your business assets is an entirely different
ballgame from the book values on your balance sheet. We'll get into
market valuing your business in Chapter 5.

2

GETTING DOWN TO DETAILS

Target The Public Offering Of Your Business For Sale To Coincide With Peak Seasons Of Business. Allow Sufficient Time To Get Your ASSET PACKAGE Ready. This Means Listing And Describing In Detail Every Tangible And Intangible Asset That You Can Come Up With. Tangible Assets Are Those Which Have Physical Size And Shape, Where Commonly Used Appraisal Techniques Are Used For Market Valuing. Intangible Assets Are Nonphysical, And Are More Elusive To Describe And Value. An Intangible Asset Must Stand Alone As An Economic Unit. Otherwise It Is Grouped In With Goodwill.

The purpose of Chapter 1 was to establish that you are serious about wanting to sell your business. The premise was that you indeed have a trade, business, or profession to sell. It is a solvent business in that you are not just one step ahead of abandonment, bankruptcy, or foreclosure. You have a reason for selling which can be presented as an opportunity to potential buyers.

Now, you have to begin the nitty-gritty details. This means that you have to define — with specificity — what it is you are going to sell. Yes, we know you are going to sell your business. But what is the business? What is its "bundle of assets": detail by detail? In other words, what exactly is the package that you are going to offer?

Your business-for-sale bundle is much more than you show on your current balance sheet. You are not ready to offer your package until you have all of your going-concern assets itemized and described in detail.

In this chapter, we want to acquaint you with the procedure for itemizing your asset package. We want to give you the broadest possible approach to the principles involved. Our contention is that you have a lot of assets that you have taken for granted over the years. The time has arrived to put them all on paper. You must do this in order to get the best sale price that you can. We want to make sure that you do not miss anything . . . in your eagerness to sell.

Set a Target Date

We all have some aversion to details, and we all tend to procrastinate. To prevent these characteristics from getting out of hand, you need to set a target date. That is, a target date when you will sign a listing contract with a nationwide property broker or advertising journal. This is the date on which you will have all your business assets fully itemized. This is also the date on which you'll have some *realistic* idea of what your pricing range should be.

Your target date should not be pulled out of the air. It should be some lead time prior to the first public offering of your business. Your first public offering should be intentionally selected to coincide with the approximate midpoint of the peak cycle of your business. All businesses have natural cycles of good seasons and slow seasons. Pick your target date for the good season time.

We are all excited when business is good; when customers are coming and going; when products and services are being sold; when money is pouring in. This same enthusiasm will be picked up by your sales broker and his buyer clients, if you time things right.

You don't want your first public offering to coincide with the down side — the slow season — of your business. Should this happen, you place yourself in the defensive position of having to explain why your business is not booming, when prospective buyers come along. You don't want this. It is always easy to explain during good times that there will be slow times. It is always difficult to explain during slow times that there will be good times.

Picking a target date requires some psychological finesse between you and your broker. He will know more about business opportunity buying cycles than you do. So, try to work out a date that is mutually satisfactory. Then advance this date by whatever time the broker or advertiser needs to get his promotional strategy on line.

We try to portray in Figure 2.1 the importance of target dating in a cyclic business. The first offering date is that on which you have the following information prepared:

1. Itemized listing of all assets for sale
2. Analysis of your business goodwill
3. Acceptable sales pricing range

We will cover goodwill and pricing separately in later chapters.

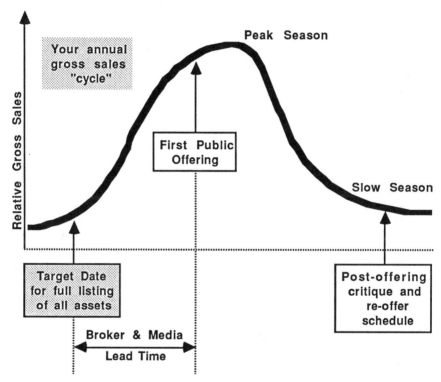

Fig. 2.1 - Setting a Target Date for Readying a Business for Sale

Land, Buildings, & Structures

Selling a business is tax classed as a *real estate transaction*. This is so, whether the business itself owns any real estate or not. It is difficult to perceive of any business not requiring the use of real estate in one manner or another. Where ownership is not involved, rents, royalties, and leases are.

As you know, real estate consists of three primary components: land, buildings, and structures. Land may be dry land, wet land, farm land, hillside land, timber land, natural resource land, etc. The term "land" includes the air space above it, the waterline around it, and the subsurface below it. In some business situations, the air space, shoreline, and subsurface portions of land are separate assets in themselves. If so, they should be identified as such: air rights, shore access, mineral rights, water rights, geothermal rights, etc.

If land is indeed an integral part of a business, such as farm land, timber land, mining land, etc., it needs to be described in terms of its surveyed acreage, location, and topography. Also, its recorded title and all amendments should be retrieved from past records and made readily available. The amount of land that is used for roadways, easements, utilities, drainage, fencing, open space, wild life refuge, etc., as applicable, should also be identified. If land is part of the business being sold, it is **the** first priority of listing in your real estate assets.

The term "building" applies to any all-weather shelter which is fitted out with necessary accommodations for human beings to live and work. There can be residential buildings, office buildings, commercial buildings, shopping malls, industrial buildings, farm houses, and the like. The amount of usable floor space in each building, its materials of construction, type of foundation, and age should be ascertained and listed. The number of floors and access features (doors, windows, elevators, ramps, loading platforms, stairways, fire escapes, etc.) should be listed as applicable. If a building has been officially inspected within the past three to five years, that fact, too, should be noted.

The term "structures" applies to attachments to land which normally are not designed to shelter people. In this category are barns, stables, storage sheds, warehouses, fuel tanks, windmills, water towers, outdoor signs, piers and docks, and the like. These, too, as applicable, should be itemized and described as part of the package of assets being offered for sale. The idea is to omit nothing of value from your asset listing.

If real estate is part of your package being offered, have all of the necessary documents at hand. This means locating your recorded title deed(s), your latest property tax bill(s), and your latest mortgage balance statement(s). The property tax bill is an especially important document because it references your APN: Assessor's

Parcel Number. This is an indexing system for publicly identifying all land in the county where your property is located. Because of the APN system, real estate is far more amenable to accurate market valuations by professional appraisers than are most other forms of business assets.

Leases & Leasehold Improvements

If your business does not consist of real estate which you own (or co-own), surely you must have a rental contract or leasing agreement with the landlord where your business is located. Rental contracts are month-to-month or year-to-year rights to use someone else's property. Leasing agreements are contracts for periods of time well over one year: 5, 10, . . . up to 99 years. Established businesses want to be sure they can stay put for a long period.

Rental contracts, because of their short-term nature, have no significant value as an asset when a business is sold. The situation is quite different for leases, however. The longer the leasing period, the longer the term remaining under the lease, the more valuable it is to a buyer. That is, providing the lease is transferable.

Suppose you had a 99-year lease on a prime commercially zoned parcel of land, on which you, and other co-owners, built various professional offices, shops, and studios. Unless the lease is transferable, there is no way that you would be able to sell your professional buildings. Any prospective buyer would want the lease along with the buildings.

Similarly for shorter term leases. Suppose you owned a beauty salon in a desirable business district of town. You have a 15-year lease, but have only used five years of it when you decide to sell your business. To a buyer, that 10 years remaining is an asset. Taking over the lease (under the same terms and conditions) is bound to save the buyer time and money. He is spared the aggravation of renegotiating the lease at a time when he has other business decisions to make.

Leasehold improvements are those made to the lessor's property (the landlord) by the lessee (the tenant). These are tangible installations such as plumbing and electrical items, equipment built-ins, fixtures, sign boards, partitions, shelving, storage areas, security systems, and other attachments to a commercial-type building. Because these improvements service the business owner's needs, and not the landlord's needs, they are paid for by the lessee.

They become the property of the landlord when the lease expires or when the lessee moves out (whichever occurs first).

Leasehold improvements are an integral part of a lessee's business operation. As such, they are a separate asset to be itemized when the business is sold. They have a value which can be determined by their original cost plus a CPI (consumer price inflation) adjustment.

There are also machinery and equipment leases in which some business owners engage. Except for built-in and bolted-down equipment, unexpired leases on movable equipment may be of little value to a potential buyer. The new owner may prefer to get his own equipment instead. The situation is quite different for built-in and bolted-down machinery and equipment. For these items, the unexpired lease terms are treated as leasehold improvements. As such, they are another asset in the business sale package.

Machinery, Equipment, & Vehicles

The term "machinery" applies to heavy duty apparatus which is mechanical and hydraulic in nature. This includes bulldozers, printing presses, machine shop lathes, generators (electrical/diesel), welding machines, tractors, farm combines, stump grinders, and the like. These are large-sized, heavy-weight items which have long-life durability. They are more subject to breakdowns and damage than to technical obsolescence. If kept repaired and operating, they are "just as good as new." Often, these are among the primary assets of a business for sale. Any potential buyer would want these items in place, as is . . . providing they are operable. Therefore, each piece of machinery (plus its accessories) should be separately described and itemized.

The term "equipment" applies more to lighter-duty items which are electrical and optical in nature. This includes all kinds of office equipment, professional tools, shop instruments, computers, oscilloscopes, power tools, air conditions, and the like. These are items subject more to technological obsolescence than to physical wear and tear. Only that equipment which has a fair market value in used condition in excess of $1,000 per item should be listed as a separate asset. Other less valuable items should either be bulk assetized or purged as junk.

The term "vehicle" applies to movable assemblies which can proceed on public highways, waterways, and airways for transporting people, produce, and products. In this category are autos, trucks, vans, trailers, boats, airplanes, and other transportative carriers. Because they are used in the public domain, each vehicle is officially licensed and registered on its own. List the registration documents in the business-offering package.

In an animal breeding business, a variant of the machinery and equipment asset category is certain "registered" animals. The female species tends to be more valuable than the male species because of the offspring it produces. The male species is valuable if it is from thoroughbred lines and has proven virility in stud services. Each quality animal, therefore, is a separate asset of its own. Its age, size, weight, and genealogy need to be itemized in the asset package. All other animals in the business for sale are common stock, which are sold either by the head or by the size of the herd.

Furniture, Fixtures, & Furnishings

Every functional business consists of a collection of furniture, fixtures, and furnishings in one form or another. Furniture, of course, consists of ordinary tables, chairs, desks, benches, cabinets, and other utilitarian items made of wood, composite, or metal. They are "ordinary" in the sense that they are not classed as equipment, such as a dental chair, or an examination table in a doctor's office.

Fixtures are such items as light fixtures, floor lamps, sign posts, toilet facilities, snack bars, time pieces, window grills, and the like. Furnishings are carpets, drapes, mirrors, wallpaper, paneling, murals, paintings, sculptures, and other esthetic items.

Unless there is some particular item or two that has stand-alone value as an antique, unusual design, or work of art, all furniture, fixtures, etc. are best treated as a bulk asset. Assign the grouping a descriptive term, and list a few examples of the types of items included. Give no detail. From a business-use point of view, these items are subject to the personal taste of the business owner. Chances are, although they might be used temporarily by the new owner, they would be ultimately replaced. Therefore, value them at some inoffensive token amount only.

As to those items which can be classed as antiques, unusual designs, or works of art, each one or each class should be separately and professionally appraised. The idea here is that if the new owner does not want them, the old owner may take them with him. He may subsequently decide to sell them separately from the asset package of the business for sale.

Materials, Supplies, & Small Tools

The term "materials" applies to raw materials and purchased parts that are used in the assembly, manufacture, and installation of tangible items for sale. The term applies to the canvas and frames used by a portrait painter; to the trimmed lumber and hinges used by a cabinet maker; to the flat bar and steel pipe used in a machine shop; or to the industrial gold and porcelain used in a dental lab. Only the *unopened* cases and packages of the materials and parts have value as an asset in a business for sale. The rationale is that the unopened containers could be returned to the original supplier for a credit on the old owner's account. Because of this direct credit potential, the unopened items are valued at their purchased cost, when included as an asset of the business for sale.

As to opened and partly used boxes of materials and parts, treat them as freebies to the new owner. The same applies to miscellaneous office and shop supplies. Small tools are all those commonly-found hand-use items in any working area. They are classed as "small" if they are operable with one hand. Include them in with the freebie supplies. Don't even try to itemize them. To itemize these as an asset of the business is an insult to a potential buyer. Assign them a token value — $100 or whatever — simply for the effort of categorizing them.

If ordinary tools require two hands for operation, such as a gasoline power saw, they are classed as large tools. Include them in with equipment, described above.

Inventory & Work in Process

The term "inventory" applies to merchandise, produce, or livestock which is ready and available for sale during daily operations of a business. "Work in process" is merchandise or products in different stages of completion, with the intention of being sold. This includes crop on the vine and young livestock which have not yet reached marketable maturity. These two terms do **not** include various materials and supplies nor anything else that a business for sale might have on hand. The terms inventory and work in process apply strictly to those finished or semifinished items that are customarily offered for sale in the ordinary course of business.

If a new owner intends to continue your business more or less as is, he definitely wants your inventory on hand at the time your business is sold. The only bone of contention likely to arise between buyer and seller is how the bulk inventory is valued. Obviously, the buyer will not pay retail price, nor will he want to pay the regular wholesale price for items which have been carried in inventory for more than one year.

When including inventory in your business-for-sale asset listing, categorize your on-hand items by type, size, nature, and when purchased. Part of this categorization process is to **purge** your inventory of damaged goods, returned merchandise, and defective items. Don't try to pass these off onto the buyer. Sell them beforehand at a clearance price, if you can, otherwise junk them. Any potential buyer only wants that of your inventory which is in first-class condition.

Accounts Receivable

Suppose that various customers/clients owe you $21,255 at the time your business changes hands. To whom do they pay: you or the new owner?

Chances are, the customers do not know that you've sold the business, particularly if the new owner continues with your same business name. So, it is immaterial to the customers. They still owe the money.

Before deciding what to do, your first consideration is to ask yourself: How long have these accounts been outstanding? To answer this question, you grade the collectibility of the accounts as follows:

Up to 30 days	—	100% collectible
30 to 60 days	—	90% collectible
60 to 90 days	—	80% collectible
Over 90 days	—	50% collectible

In most solvent businesses, accounts due for over 90 days are treated as 50/50 in their collectibility. The affected customers are having financial and other personal difficulties. Unless an over-90-day customer is able to explain his situation and intentions, you can only assume that you have a 50/50 chance of collecting. Most customers willingly pay their bills within 30, 60, or 90 days.

Having graded your accounts receivable as above, suppose you compute your overall collectibility of the $21,255 above to be $16,212. (Bear in mind that this is just an example.) Now, what do you do about the $16,212? It certainly is a tangible asset to a new owner, if he were to collect it. Therefore, one approach is to list it as such in your asset package with all backup details (the name of each customer, the amount he owes, the invoice date of your billing him).

Another approach is to consider *your* accounts payable as an offset against your accounts receivable. We are dealing here only with your *business trade* accounts: money you owe to suppliers, vendors, tradesmen, etc. Since you are a solvent business, it is presumed that you pay these accounts within 30 days. With this in mind, let's assume that your trade accounts payable total $10,212 (just for example).

Why not propose to the new owner that you be allowed to offset your graded accounts receivable of $16,212 by the $10,212 trade accounts payable? This way, the net asset that you are selling to the buyer is:

Accounts receivable *less* accounts payable = $6,000

This way, also, when the buyer takes over, he — not you — pays off your outstanding trade accounts. In return, the buyer gets *all* of your accounts receivable . . . even if he is able to collect more than the $16,212 you computed.

Tangible Assets Summarized

A tangible asset is something that can be seen, felt, and heard. It has physical size, shape, and color. It can be weighed and measured. As such, it can be realistically valued in the market place through professional appraisers, comparable sales, second-hand dealers, and replacement costing. Some estimations are involved but no mystique is required.

One of the first things that a serious prospective buyer wants to know is what all of your tangible assets are worth. He knows that when he buys tangibles, he's going to get something specific for his money. He can compare your values with other tangibles he may have or have access to. He can sense, feel, and compare those tangible assets that you have listed in detail for him. This is **not** the case with intangible assets.

Your listing of tangible assets (those which we have described above), become the rock solid foundation price of the business which you are offering for sale. It is the base on which you build the pricing of your intangible assets. The intangible assets in one business are very difficult to compare with similar intangibles in another business. This is because of the emotional attachment that owners have with intangibles. Tangible assets generally are quite emotion-free.

Because of the foundation nature of tangible assets, we summarize "all of the above" for you in Figure 2.2. The purpose of this figure is to provide you with a checklist for classifying your own assets which you are going to offer up for sale. Obviously, not all items shown will pertain to your business. But some may be applicable which you have not thought about before.

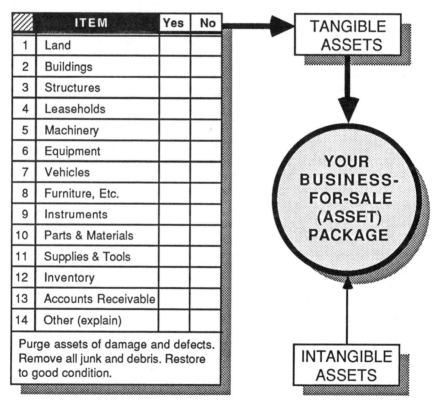

Fig. 2.2 - Checklist Summary of Tangible Assets

In addition to tangible assets, a solvent business consists also of intangible assets. These are more elusive to describe and value, because they are nonphysical in form. Examples are franchises, trademarks, patents, copyrights, trade names, customer lists, covenants not to compete, and so on. We want to touch on these items below because some, invariably, will apply to your particular business. Intangibles become your "bargaining chips" for pricing your business over and above that which your tangible assets would produce on their own.

Precautions With Franchises

For some small businesses, the principal intangible asset often is a franchise. A franchise is an agreement whereby the franchisee has the right to distribute, sell, or provide goods, services, or facilities of the franchisor within a specific geographic area. The right may be exclusive or nonexclusive. It is an exclusive right if the franchisee is limited to promoting only the franchisor's line of products or services. It is a nonexclusive right if the franchisee can promote other products or services which are not in direct competition with the franchisor's items. Thus, when you are ready to sell your business, you are cautioned to restudy your franchise agreement . . . and all of its technicalities.

Franchises are created by corporate entities who prefer to have a unique line of products or services for which there is widespread public demand. The franchisors want to expand their outlets nationwide, without putting up their own money to do so. Consequently, they actively solicit franchisees to put up the money to conduct a local business in an independent manner. This way, the franchisor has an assured outlet for his products/services; the franchisee has an assured nationally known line of products/services to distribute or sell.

There are legal technicalities in a franchise agreement which many small business owners do not fully understand. What it all boils down to is that a franchisee does not acquire outright ownership of the franchise which he pays for. Instead, he acquires a *license* to use the franchisor's trade name and trademark for distributing/selling the franchisor's products/services. Under the licensing principles, the franchisor retain certain ownership rights and continuing interest in the franchised items.

What this all means is that when you are ready to sell your business, including your franchise license, you have to notify and consult with the franchisor. When you do, the fine print in your agreement *may* permit him to terminate the franchise. If this happens, it could kill the potential sale of your business. However, most franchisors want their products/services to continue being distributed/sold. So, they will cooperate with you in making the franchise transition to a new owner. They may even provide leads on potential buyers who have contacted the home office for geographic regions similar to, or near, yours.

When you sell your franchise license along with your other business assets, you will have a cost basis in it. That basis will be the total cost you paid for the franchise *less* any amortization of cost that you may have taken on your tax return (called: adjusted cost). Your pricing of the franchise to your buyer may be higher than, or lower than, your adjusted cost. Much depends on the success of the franchised business in the area you have served.

Patents and Copyrights

Some small businesses are founded upon products or services which arise from patents or copyrights. Often, the business owner himself, or in in conjunction with one or two others, is the creator. Or the patent or copyright may have been purchased from other creators. Either way, these are special assets of the business and need to be valued as such.

A patent is granted by the U.S. Patent Office for technology-type inventions and process formulas. A copyright is granted by the U.S. Copyright Office for literary, historical, and artistic works. A patent is good for 17 years (renewable), whereas a copyright is good for the life of the author plus 50 years.

The cost of a patent or copyright consists of various government fees; the costs of drawings, molds, and patterns; legal fees and other similar expenditures. Thus, each patent or copyright that you use in your business has a determinable cost of its own. This is particularly the case if, as the creator, you take into account the amount of time you devoted to its creation.

If your business is patent- or copyright-dependent, you have a decision to make when you sell the business. Do you sell the patent(s) or copyright(s) with the business? Or do you license their use by the new owner? Much depends on your personal sensitivity (if you are the creator), and on the expectations of the prospective buyer.

If you decide to sell your patent or copyright, you need to project an income stream for it . . . 5 to 10 years out. Projecting an income stream this far tends to be speculative at best. Nevertheless, if you have some past income history, reasonable projections can be made. Once the projections are accepted by the buyer, you price your patent or copyright at some fixed percentage thereof: typically, in the range of 10% or so.

If the projections of income from your patent or copyright are too risky for a buyer, he may opt instead for a licensing agreement with you. The buyer then pays you royalties based on some fixed or variable percentage of the income which he receives.

Licenses and Permits

If you have obtained a license or permit from a public agency, and you use that license or permit in your business, here again you have an asset that can be sold. Included in this category are registrations and inspections by government agencies. All of these have some value to a prospective buyer. It depends on the type of document issued and the duration remaining to regular expiration.

A license may be general or specific. A general business license has no value to a buyer of the business, as he has to get one for himself immediately after your sale anyhow. The only value of such a license is that it helps to verify that you are indeed the legitimate operator of the business being sold.

A specific license such as a liquor license, cigarette license, or firearms license, often has buyer value in excess of that of its original cost. This is particularly true where said licenses are restricted in the number officially issued in a given area. If there is a run on firearm purchases in a high crime area, for example, the firearms license to a business owner near that area is certainly higher in value than that of a similar business owner in a low crime neighborhood. Liquor licenses have traditionally been highly prized assets for small business operators.

A permit is local authority to build or install specific items at a specific location or locations. Most permits automatically expire when the intended work is completed. If there is work yet to be completed that you were to perform, and it is completed by the buyer who derives the income from doing so, the related unexpired permits definitely have value. The buyer would be spared the cost of getting a new permit on his own. In restricted-growth metropolitan areas, building-type permits are costly.

Registrations are public listings of vehicles that use public highways, waterways, and airways. If transferable, unexpired registrations have pro rata value to buyers who acquired your vehicles for continued business use. Intra- and inter-state trucking registrations are extremely expensive. They are thus valuable assets in any small trucking business being offered for sale.

Recently completed official inspections are also valuable assets. Particularly if they relate to building inspections, safety inspections, fire inspections, health inspections, hazardous waste inspections, environmental inspections, and so on. Valuing these as separate assets relates directly to the cost, time, and materials of preparing for the inspections, and to the cost for correcting any citation defects.

Contracts and Easements

If you have contracts for others to perform work for you, or for you to perform work for others, and the contracts are active, they are assets to your business at time of its sale. Your first task for listing them as such is to gather up all of the actual signed documents. Arrange them into two categories, namely: "contracts in" and "contracts out." Exclude from this effort work in process which is part of your inventory that we discussed earlier.

The term "contracts in" means those which provide products or services to you. These arrangements include employment contracts, maintenance contracts, security contracts, vendor contracts, insurance contracts, and the like. These are specific items which you can add to your listing of assets. They are assets in the sense that effort has been expended on your part to consummate them. This effort is worth something to a buyer, if he intends to continue with the same contractees. The value to him would be some reasonable hourly rate for your time. A range of from 15% to 35% of that rate might be appropriate for saving the buyer's time on the same consummation effort.

The term "contracts out" includes those arrangements where your business is to provide products or services over an extended period of time at a contractually established price. These arrangements provide you a source of income that you can count on. When performance is made, they constitute money in your hands. They are also money in the buyer's hands if you turn those contracts over to him.

What are they worth to you — and to a prospective buyer? If you or the buyer were to pay a salesperson to go out and drum up those contracts out, what commission would you pay him? Probably in the 10% to 15% range? The asset value of these contracts would be the total to-be-performed value times the commission percentage that you and the buyer agree upon.

An easement is the purchase of rights to use someone else's property for better access to your business premises. We're referring to private easements: not to public nor utility easements. Through a private contract you bought access rights over your neighbor's property. Presumably, if you sell your business, the new owner would want those same access rights, too. Said rights are an asset to be listed in your business package.

Customer Lists

There is one asset category of your business that a prospective buyer definitely wants. He wants your customer lists. He wants a list of all those customers with whom you've done business within the past three years. He wants them broken down year by year: the most recent year first, the second most recent year, and the third year. For each year, for each customer's account, he wants the gross dollar amount of product or services bought. This information alone will give the buyer a true handle on what kind of income stream he might expect, after taking over your business.

Yes, we know there's a lot of detail and record-sorting to do to get all of this information together. It is important to keep in mind that your customer list is the *most persuasive* intangible asset of your business. As long as your listing of accounts is real, and you have purged it of nonpaying and late-paying customers (those paying after 90 days), you have bargaining statistics which are hard to refute.

Most buyers of businesses know that former customers do not always return when a new owner takes over. Many do, however, out of sheer force of habit and convenience. This means that all customer lists have two components: a self-regenerating component and a wasting component. These two components can be sorted out through samplings of selected customers over a 3-, 5-, 10-year history . . . or for however long you have been in business.

How do you value a customer list?

You use the sales commission approach. For example, suppose the annual average of three years of gross sales comes to $100,000 What commission would you — or the buyer — be willing to pay a sales person to generate this amount of business: 10%, 15% . . .? Once you come to an agreement on this figure (which is for one average year of sales), you then apply a "self-regenerating" multiplying factor for repetitive sales year after year. This, then, would be what your customer lists are worth.

Intangible Assets Summarized

In our discussion above, we have not included every conceivable intangible asset possible. Large businesses have other buyer-wanted intangibles such as: trademarks, trade names, company logos, package designs, advertising slogans, computer software, inventory accounting methods, covenants not to compete, and other proprietary items. Small businesses rarely have these sophisticated items. If your business does, certainly add it to the asset listing in your business-for-sale package.

We want to summarize in Figure 2.3 what we believe are the most likely applicable intangible assets for a small business owner. You may treat it as a checklist reminder of what not to overlook when preparing your business for sale.

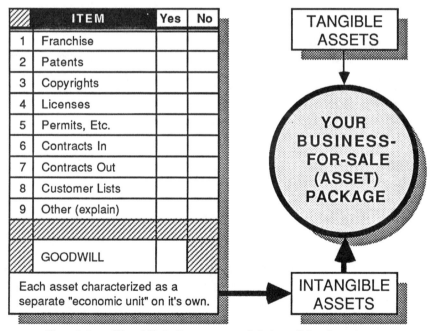

Fig. 2.3 - Checklist Summary of Intangible Assets

Here's a special point to keep in mind about intangible assets. Unlike a piece of machinery or equipment, an intangible asset has no inherent self-evident value of its own. Its value is derived from experience and other factors of the business. This means that the seller himself has to extract from his own experience those features which he believes make each intangible asset valuable to a buyer. In other words, each intangible asset has to stand on its own as a *separate economic reality*. This is why, for example, we stressed customer lists above.

Unless an intangible asset can be convincingly portrayed as a separate economic unit of its own, it is "thrown in" with the overall concept of goodwill.

For example, suppose you operate a lawn care business with your own name and logo. You call yourself: "Magic Bubbler Lawn Care." You designed an attractive logo of a bubbler-type tool dispensing water, air, fertilizer, and weed killer in a range of mixing ratios You are not affiliated with any regional or national organization generally known to the public. Your name and logo are purely proprietary items of your own. When you sell your business, can you really claim that your name and logo are a separate economic unit of their own?

Without the other attributes of your business, would your name and logo themselves sell in the national marketplace? Probably not. Consequently, when you sell your business, your name and logo become part of the goodwill that you sell to the buyer . . . for a price. It is the *goodwill* that you sell: not your name and logo.

3

DETERMINING GOODWILL

Goodwill Is The Expectancy Of Continued Patronage From Existing Customers After A Business Is Sold. This Patronage Evolves From The INTANGIBLES Of A Business: Rarely From Tangibles. Tangible Assets Become The Computational Basis For Determining "Industry Average Earnings" Of The Business. Excess Earnings, If Any, Are Attributable To Goodwill. A 4-Step INCOME CAPITALIZATION Procedure — Called: The Formula Method — Is Used. From The "Formula Value" Of Goodwill, Computed Values Of Franchises, Patents, Copyrights, Licenses, Contracts, & Customer Lists Are Subtracted To Arrive At Your "Adjusted" Goodwill.

It is said that every solvent business has goodwill . . . more or less. In competitive businesses with similar products and services, some seem to have more goodwill than others. Their customers seem to keep coming back, and, through word-of-mouth referrals, encourage other customers to do so. What is it that makes one business stand out from another in the same field of endeavor? Is there some mystique involved?

Yes, apparently so, but it is not always as mysterious as one might think. If you search hard enough, you may find some underlying feature in the business which makes it stand apart from its competitors. It may have something to do with the particular tangible assets it has, or with certain of its intangibles. It has something to do with the "chemistry" between the business operator and the niche public that he serves.

This raises the question then: How do you determine the elements of the business that generate the goodwill, and how do you value it? Do you just pull a dollar figure out of the air, then leave it up to the buyer and seller to thrash out their differences of opinion? If you do this — pull a goodwill figure out of the air — the IRS will say that your goodwill is zero.

There is no clear-cut proven method for determining and valuing goodwill. There are several responsible approaches, and these are what we want to cover in this chapter. It is obvious — or should be — that you cannot separate goodwill from the rest of your business and treat it as an asset of its own. Yet, this is what the IRS tries to do in its pecking-order system of hindsight after a sale is consummated. Yet, you need to know, *before* the sale of your business, what your goodwill consists of and what its value should be. We'll try to provide you with some guidelines in this regard.

Pertinent Generalizations

Goodwill stems primarily from the intangible assets of a business. Rarely does any tangible asset — such as a building, a piece of machinery, some special tool or equipment, or the latest computer update — create any air of goodwill on its own. It is the intangibles — not all of them necessarily — that create goodwill and customer satisfaction.

It may be type of employees and management style; it may be the "catchiness" of advertising and promotional effort; it may be the physical location and cleanliness of the business premises; it may be the use of trademarks, copyrights, patents, and franchises; it may be the convenient hours of operation; it may be the owner's reputation for skill, affluence, or punctuality; or it may be that old-fashioned attitude that "the customer is nearly always right." Whatever it is, it is there.

Goodwill is not expressly reflected in financial statements of the business other than the fact that the owner's return on investment may be above the industry average. Thus, one measure of goodwill is the "excess earnings" of the business when compared with other businesses of equally competitive nature. The net effect is that there appears to be some distinct advantage or benefit that a business enjoys, which is over and above that of the physical assets themselves.

For small businesses, goodwill is defined as that value which is at least equal to the total capital a new business would require to get where the established business is today. This implies that goodwill is the excess capital required over and above the replacement value of all separately identified assets of the existing business.

The generally accepted meaning of goodwill is—

The expectancy of continued patronage from existing customers without contractual compulsion. This patronage is inseparable from the business itself.

In Figure 3.1, we depict our version of goodwill as it relates to a small business for sale. The underlying thesis is that each asset — tangible or intangible — which can be separately identified as a potentially salable economic unit of its own be identified and valued first. That which remains inseparable from the business package as a whole is goodwill.

Early Tax Decisions

The dollar value of goodwill becomes a major bone of contention between buyer and seller, *after* the sale has been consummated. This is because the IRS comes on the scene several years later to "juggle the terms" of the contract in a way that produces the maximum tax revenue. It is the buyer who suffers most in this regard A thoughtful seller, therefore, should try to formulate his goodwill pricing in a manner that will best stand up to any post-sale litigation by the buyer. Towards this end, we'd like to review with you some early Tax Court decisions on goodwill matters.

The concept of goodwill for tax allocation purposes goes back to the early 1930's. One of the earliest cases on record was that of *J. Gumpel*, 2 BTA 1127. In *Gumpel*, the court ruled that:

*Goodwill is not confined to a name. It may be attached to a particular locality where the business is transacted, to a list of customers, or to other elements of value in business as a going concern. **It cannot be transferred separately**. [Emphasis added.]*

In another early case, *C.J. Tsivoglou*, 3 BTA 743, the court ruled that:

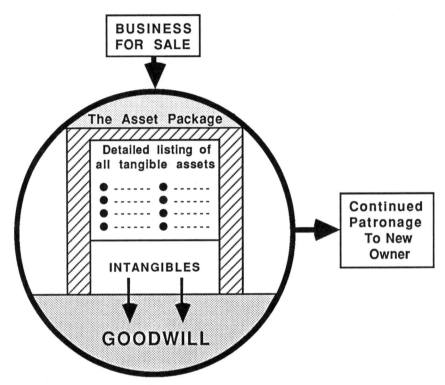

Fig. 3.1 - Inseparability of Goodwill from the Business Package

*The value of goodwill by capitalizing excess earnings may be disproved by showing the **business was insolvent** at the valuation date, despite prior large earnings.* [Emphasis added.]

The arbitrary allocation of a dollar amount to goodwill will not fly. One of the very earliest Tax Court cases establishes this point quite clearly. In *Farmers Grain Co.*, 1 BTA 605, the court concluded:

*A taxpayer purchased a going grain elevator plan including goodwill, but did not set up on its books any goodwill account. In **absence of evidence of existence** of goodwill or of its value, arbitrary allocation of a portion of the purchase price to goodwill was disallowed.* [Emphasis added.]

In another ruling, *V.J. McQuade*, 4 BTA 837, the court held:

Average annual earnings and average tangible assets as shown by the books, standing alone, does not prove existence of goodwill.

And in still another case, *R.J. Durkee*, 8 TCM 701, the court found:

Since expenditures to develop goodwill may have been deducted as a current expense, as indicated by the fact that no goodwill account was kept, goodwill was found to have a zero basis.

What the *Durkee* case shows is that the seller of a business has no recorded reference basis for establishing goodwill. An exception would have been had the current seller purchased the business from a prior owner to whom he paid an amount for goodwill, and carried that amount on his books as a capital asset. Otherwise, every seller is on his own to establish that his business has a determinable amount of goodwill.

No Natural Endowment

There is no requirement in the tax code that, when a business is sold, there be an element of goodwill associated therewith. Businesses can be sold without goodwill. In fact, for small businesses this is often the case in reality. Businesses which have only been in existence for a few years rarely can be said to have been around long enough to establish any goodwill. The common knowledge is that goodwill is largely determined by reference to the long prior history and continued prosperity of the business.

Early courts have ruled [*Aetna Sprinkler Co.*, 15 BTA 521] that a solvent business in existence for only two years has no goodwill. Similarly, other courts have ruled [*Magnus, Mabee, Inc.* 1 BTA 907] that where the return on owner's capital is below average, there is no goodwill even when operating for five years. These early cases pretty well prescribe the number of years in business as being from three to five years before the economic reality of goodwill trips in. Even then, goodwill applies only to better-than-average businesses.

Regardless of one's length of time in business, if operating an ordinary type activity in a highly competitive area, there still may be no goodwill. This was the position taken in the Tax Court case of *P. Vamvaks*, 4 TCM 733. That court held:

Goodwill was not a factor in determining gain from complete liquidation of a laundry where goodwill had no market value because of the highly competitive nature of such business in the vicinity.

The case law above is clear that goodwill is not an endowment of every business simply because the owner has stayed with it for several years.

So, why do small businesses even try to establish a goodwill factor when selling their business? It has something to do with refusing to accept that the business was not all that successful. By putting a little goodwill in the pricing formula, it conveys the subliminal message to the buyer that the business has great potential in the buyer's hands. In this sense, goodwill represents a profit bonus to the entrepreneur who painstakingly got the business started.

Covenant Not to Compete

Small businesses — because they are small — are very sensitive to competition from similar businesses in their general vicinity. When buying a business, therefore, the buyer wants assurance that the former owner will not turn around and start up a "new improved" business nearby. This is where a covenant not to compete comes in.

A covenant is an agreement by the seller not to compete with the buyer in a similar or near-similar business for a term of years certain. The most common covenant time is five years. This gives the new owner adequate time to put his own stamp on the business and develop a goodwill factor of his own. If it can withstand an IRS challenge, a covenant also permits the buyer to amortize the cost of the covenant over the 5-year contract period. Thus, from the seller's point of view, a covenant is a form of goodwill created on the spot. It is an accommodation to the buyer to induce him to buy. It is clearly an intangible asset to the business being sold.

On the subject of goodwill as an intangible, in 1956 the IRS adopted Regulation 1.167(a)-3: Intangibles. In substance, this regulation says—

If an intangible asset is known from experience or other factors to be of use in the business or in the production of income for only a limited period, the length of which can be estimated with reasonable accuracy, such an intangible asset may be the subject of a depreciation [or amortization] allowance. . . . No allowance will be permitted merely because, in the unsupported opinion of the taxpayer, the intangible asset has a limited useful life.

This regulatory wording seems to condone the concept of goodwill in the form of a covenant not to compete. But does it? Various cases are used by the IRS to attack any covenant between seller and buyer which, in its opinion—

has no basis in economic reality.

The IRS takes the position that the "mere forbearance from competition" is really goodwill under a different name. Said forbearance is a necessary adjunct to goodwill, and is indeed inseparable from it. This is because such covenant is essential to assure the buyer the beneficial enjoyment of the goodwill he has acquired. As such, the covenant is nonseverable and not subject to depreciation/amortization.

On the other hand, where the buyer would not have been willing to purchase the business without the covenant and would not have paid the price he did unless the covenant were included, it has been held that the covenant could be segregated and depreciated/amortized. To establish this segregation, however, the burden of proof is on the buyer. He must employ the "economic substance test" whereby the noncompetition was a necessity of the business. This would be difficult to show where the seller was retiring from business, or was moving out of state.

What does all the above say?

It says that if a small business lacks any specific intangible asset with respect to which goodwill can be determined, it can create a covenant not to compete, and use the agreed dollar amount as a measure of the goodwill. That is, provided the facts and circumstances truly warrant such a covenant. After all, if the buyer insists that he needs the protection of a covenant, and the seller agrees . . . for a price, can the IRS come in after the fact, and change things around? Sadly, it often tries.

Income Capitalization Approach

For businesses that have been in existence five years or more, the IRS will consider allowing what is called the "income capitalization" method for determining goodwill. This method adopts an average annual rate of return (of 8% to 10%) on the tangible assets of a business. This amount is deducted from the pretax earnings of the business. The remainder or "excess earnings" is capitalized (at 15% to 20%) to arrive at a *formula value* of the intangible assets of the business. If the intangibles cannot be separately valued on their own — such as patents, copyrights, customer lists — the formula amount becomes the computed goodwill.

The IRS's formula approach to goodwill is set forth in its Revenue Ruling 68-609, 1968-2CB327. Though a 1968 ruling, this approach can still be used today if no better determination method is applicable. Selected excerpts from this reference document are as follows:

The 8% rate of return and the 15% rate of capitalization are applied to tangibles and intangibles, respectively, of businesses with small risk factors and stable and regular earnings. The 10% rate of return and the 20% rate of capitalization are applied to businesses in which the hazards of business are relatively high.

The past earnings to which the formula is applied should fairly reflect the probably future earnings. Ordinarily, the period should not be less than 5 years, and abnormal years, whether above or below the average, should be eliminated. If the business is a sole proprietorship or partnership, there should be deducted from the earnings of the business a reasonable amount for services performed by the owner or partners.

Only the tangible assets entering into net worth, including trade accounts receivable in excess of trade accounts payable, are used for determining earnings on the tangible assets.

The IRS's formula approach should **not** be used if there is better evidence available from which the value of intangibles can be determined. Furthermore, the approach is not valid where the fair market value of the tangible assets is greater than the actual selling price of the business. Limitations apply where it is obvious that there are no intangibles of value to the business.

4-Step Formula Process

An understanding of the formula (income capitalization) method of arriving at goodwill is a prelude to understanding other techniques for pricing your business. It is the *methodology* that is important: not necessarily the results obtained. The method requires a 4-step process of analysis and computation.

Step 1: Determine the *average* book value of your tangible assets over the most recent five years of your business. Use your existing books of account and financial statements. Tangible assets comprise all of your capital assets, depreciable assets, amortizable assets, and net cash flow (cash on hand plus net of current receivables over current payables). For illustration purposes, you arrive at a figure of $100,000. This is the average capital investment you have in your business, as reflected by your own books. No estimates or appraisals are involved.

Step 2: Adopt an industry average rate of return for businesses similar to yours. Be realistic, get comparables where you can. The range is probably 6% to 10%. Let's use 8%. Multiply the $100,000 of invested capital by the 8% to arrive at $8,000 ($100,000 x 0.08). In theory, this is the income earned on capital by an average business of your type. It is analogous to the rate of return you would expect, if you put the same amount of capital into a passive investment, instead of in your own active business.

Step 3: Look at the net earnings statement of your business for the current year (for which you are valuing goodwill). Subtract out your depreciation/amortization deduction, if any. This gives you your *pretax* net earnings. Let's assume this figure is $20,000. Now, subtract the average industry earnings of $8,000 from your pretax earnings of $20,000. You arrive at $12,000 ($20,000 - $8,000). This is your "excess earnings" relative to your adopted industry average.

Step 4: Select a capitalization rate depending on the risks and volatility of your business. This could range from 10% for very low risk businesses, to 20% for high risk businesses. Let's use 15%. Now "capitalize" the $12,000 excess earnings by dividing it by the 15% or 0.15. The result is

$$\frac{\$12,000}{0.15} = \$80,000$$

The $80,000 figure is the formula computed value of *all* of your intangible assets. Unless you can reconstruct by other means one or more of your intangible assets, this becomes the goodwill value of all of your intangibles.

We summarize the above four steps in Figure 3.2. They illustrate the type of computational effort that is required in order to avoid allegations of arbitrariness and guessing when you price your goodwill.

For Businesses In Existence 5 Years Or More	
1	Determine average book value of all tangible assets (including intangibles carried regularly on books).
2	Adopt industry average rate of return on book valued assets (6% to 10%). Multiply by step 1.
3	Determine pretax earnings (BEFORE depreciation/amortization allowances) for current business year. Subtract step 2.
4	Select a capitalization rate (10% to 20%) appropriate to risks & volatility of business. Divide into step 3. Obtain "Formula Goodwill"

Fig. 3.2 - The 4-Step Sequence for "Formula Computing" Goodwill

Those "Separable" Intangibles

The formula method above produces a figure that represents the collective goodwill of all the intangibles of the business. We know from our discussions in Chapter 2 that some intangibles can be separated from goodwill and valued on their own. This is certainly the case for such items as franchises, patents, copyrights, licenses, contracts, drawings, leases, customer lists, and the like. Where appropriate, and where such items can be separated as an economic unit, they should be separated. As a practical rule of thumb, the economic separation should not be made where the reconstructed value of an intangible item turns out to be less than $1,000.

There are various methods for computing the value of a separable intangible, such as: cost-of-purchase, cost-savings, cost-to-create, etc. The point we want to make here is that once a value is computed, that value — or total of several values — is *subtracted* from the collective formula value to arrive at an "adjusted" goodwill value. This adjusted goodwill concept is presented in Figure 3.3.

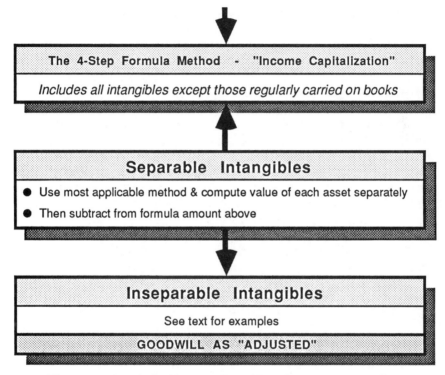

Fig. 3.3 - Goodwill Derived From The "Formula Method"

For example, suppose you were able to show that your copyright is worth $50,000. Subtracting this amount from the $80,000 collective goodwill above, leaves your adjusted (inseparable) goodwill items at $30,000 ($80,000 - $50,000).

Intangible items which are generally inseparable from goodwill are:

1. Startup losses already absorbed by the business.
2. Trained employees and their attentiveness to customers.
3. Advertising and promotional effort already undertaken.
4. The location of property, plant, and equipment.

5. General reputation of the business and its owner(s)
6. Accounting systems and other internal controls in place.
7. Prompt and fair-minded customer relations.
8. Occasional media appearances of owner(s) and manager(s)

Once you have determined and valued your separable intangibles — those worth $1,000 or more each — there is no point in even itemizing the inseparables. Gross everything else in with goodwill and let it go at that.

Profit-Opportunity Method

If you really think you have some creative genius in your business — some intangible asset that will last for years and years (such as a patent or copyright) — the profit-opportunity method of computing goodwill is for you. This method involves projecting an average annual income stream at least 10 years out. The projections are based on the past five years, taking into account incremental increases in income from year to year.

For example, consider that you have a copyright on a financial book or computer software program. You faithfully update it every three years or so, expecting that the sales of your production units will go on and on. You are able to isolate from your income records those proceeds which arise directly from your copyrighted item. Your records show this income to be:

Year 1	$ 6,000)	
Year 2	8,000)	
Year 3	9,000)	45,000 ÷ 5 yrs
Year 4	10,000)	= $9,000/yr average
Year 5	12,000)	
Total	$45,000	

You note that, in the most recent year, sales increased 20% over the prior year. So, instead of using $9,000 per year average, you decide to use $10,000. You look in the present-value tables in an accounting handbook, and note that the present-value (P.V.) factor for 10 years at an 8% rate of return per year is 6.710.

From the information above, the computed goodwill on your copyright would be

$10,000/yr x 6.710 P.V. for 10 yrs = $67,100

Priority	ASSET	NATURE	COMMENT
1	Cash & cash equivalents	Current cash	Include accounts receivable < 30 days *
2	Marketable securities, loans, & notes	Discounted cash	Loans & accounts receivable < 1 year **
3	Inventory & work in process	Merchandise for sale	Use conservative accounting
4	Land, buildings, & leaseholds	Real estate	Get professional appraisals
5	Machinery, vehicles, & equipment	Tangibles, large	Get second-hand dealer appraisals
6	Furniture, fixtures, & instruments	Tangibles, other	Get second-hand dealer appraisals
7	Materials, supplies, small tools, etc.	Bulk tangibles	Original cost, highly discounted
8	Franchises, copyrights, licenses, contracts, etc.	Separable intangibles	Compute with most applicable method
9	Staff & procedural items of "going concern"	Inseparable intangibles	Use "formula" & subtract item 8
		* offset with payables < 30 days	
		** offset with payables < 1 year	

Fig. 3.4 - Prioritizing of Assets for Residual Goodwill

If your projections are right on, the buyer would derive $100,000 from your copyright ($10,000/yr x 10 yrs). If your projections were high, he might derive only $80,000 (at $8,000/yr); if they were low, he might derive $120,000 (at $12,000/yr). Either way, the buyer gets the benefit of your projection errors.

The Residual (Hindsight) Method

No matter what method you use, or how reasonable you try to be, the IRS can come on the scene two to three years after the sale of your business . . . to "switch things around." It does this under its *residual method* of determining your goodwill. Basically, this method is one of scrutinizing everything else first, then what's left over — if anything — is treated as goodwill.

The residual method is used **after** the sale price is known. This is the "hindsight approach" which the IRS is famous for. For an owner preparing for sale, there is no hindsight he can use. He has to move forward with trying to price-tag his business the best way that he can.

Nevertheless, even before sale, it is instructive to review the hindsight method that the IRS uses. It is predicated upon prioritizing in valuation categories all business-for-sale assets in descending order of controversy. That is, the least controversial assets are listed first; the most controversial are listed last . . . just before goodwill. The value of goodwill is the very last listing. It could turn out to be zero!

For example, cash on hand (or in the bank) on a specific date is a noncontroversial value. It is a book entry, computer entry, or cash register entry of so many dollars. There are no assumptions or computational methodology required. If the entries are genuine, there is no equivocation over value involved. At the other end of the prioritizing categories, separable intangible assets do engender equivocation and controversy.

We list in Figure 3.4 the prioritizing sequence of asset categories that go into the residual method analysis. We have inserted a few comments alongside each category, so that you might sense the extent of controversy that could arise. As you proceed down the list, more and more computational assumptions and judgment calls have to be made.

Wherever applicable, spend the money necessary to get professional appraisals, comparable pricings, and third-party statements concerning your asset values. Do your homework and prepare a bound data book on your value listings; include all backup documents. Believe us, doing your homework now — before the business is sold — will save you much aggravation and second thoughts after it is sold. A well-prepared asset-value book is itself an item of goodwill to your buyer.

4

NEW RULES ON INTANGIBLES

A Major Change Took Place In 1993 Affecting The Valuation And Treatment Of Goodwill And Its Related Intangibles. Section 197 Was Enacted Which Mandated That Goodwill, Etc. Be Amortized Over 15 Years. Thus, A New Category of Business Assets Was Created, Called: **AMORTIZABLE SECTION 197 INTANGIBLES.** Some 10 Items Are Expressly Included, When Acquired In Connection With The Sale, Merger, Or Change Of Ownership Of A "Going Concern" Business. This New Category Is Valued By Using The "Residual Method" . . . Once The Gross Sale Price Of A Business Is Known.

Since 1956, the IRS has held steadfastly to its position that goodwill and its associated intangibles was a pure capital asset. This meant that, once acquired, the goodwill, etc. could not be depreciated or amortized over time. It had indeterminable life, which to the IRS it meant that it had indefinite life . . . like land.

To a seller who had created the goodwill, etc., the IRS position was not of great concern. But, to the buyer, the IRS position meant locked-up capital for many, many years. The goodwill and its intangibles represented money which the buyer had paid for, but which he could never recover from the operation of the business that he had bought. Any cost recovery to the buyer only occurred when he resold the business to another buyer.

The situation changed in 1993 with the Revenue Reconciliation Act of that year. Congress finally got tired of the IRS's intransigence. It added a new section to the Internal Revenue Code, namely: **Section 197**. Unfortunately, it took Congress many years to come to its senses. The wave of mergers and acquisitions sweeping across Corporate America in the 1980's caused hundreds of millions of dollars to be tied up in goodwill capital that could not be used for generating jobs. Congress tried to correct this situation with its new Section 197 added to the federal tax code. The new section permits the amortization of goodwill and certain other intangibles over a 15-year period. This new law is effective for all business acquisitions taking place after August 10, 1993.

Because of the importance of this issue to a prospective buyer of your business, we want to address in this chapter the background and features of Section 197. While this new law does not change the valuation concepts presented in Chapter 3, it does enable the seller to better understand the motivation and resistance of the buyer to whatever value is placed on goodwill and its nonseparable intangibles. There has been a long-fought history against the IRS by large corporate buyers of businesses. This all came to a head in the U.S. Supreme Court on April 20, 1993.

The High Court Ruling

Congress did not decide to do something about goodwill and intangibles on its own. It should have. It had enough forewarning from Corporate America. It was not until the Newark Morning Ledger, a newspaper publisher, appealed to the U.S. Supreme Court — and won — that Congress finally came up with its new Section 197.

The case of *Newark Morning Ledger Co. v. U.S.* is a milestone and landmark in the long history of business owners trying to implant reasonableness and common sense in the IRS bureaucracy. For tax historians, this case is cited as—

S Ct, 93-1 USTC ¶ 50,228
rev'g and rem'g CA-3, 91-2 USTC ¶ 50,451

Here, the abbreviations are: S Ct is Supreme Court; USTC is U.S. Tax Cases; rev'g and rem'g is reversing and remanding; CA-3 is U.S. Court of Appeals for the Third Circuit. The term "remand" means to send back to a lower court for additional proceedings.

In the cited case, the Court of Appeals (CA-3) ruled in favor of the IRS [945 F2d 555]. It did so by reversing and remanding a

U.S. District Court (District of New Jersey) decision [734 F Supp 176] which ruled against the IRS. By reversing and remanding the Court of Appeals decision, the Supreme Court reinstated the findings and conclusions of the District Court. The District Court ruled on April 3, 1990 that the plaintiff, the Newark Morning Ledger Company—

was entitled to depreciate the corresponding adjusted tax basis of the paid subscribers of the acquired newspapers as of the date of liquidation and merger, on a straight-line basis over their stipulated useful lives.

How much money was involved in the paid subscriber goodwill accounts?

Answer: $67,773,000!

This was the "low figure" presented to the Court by several financial and statistical experts. The useful life estimates ranged from 14.7 years for daily subscribers to 23.4 years for Sunday subscribers. Altogether, the Newark Company through a series of 16 mergers and acquisitions had acquired the names and addresses of 913,713 paid subscribers.

To tie up nearly 68 million dollars as a nonrecoverable capital asset, as the IRS would have done, is devastating to the profitability of any business. Fortunately, the High Court may have sensed this.

The essence of the High Court's ruling is as follows:

Petitioner has borne successfully its substantial burden of proving that "paid subscribers" constitutes an intangible asset with an ascertainable value and a limited useful life, the duration of which can be ascertained with reasonable accuracy. It has proved that the asset is not self-regenerating but wastes, as a finite number of component subscriptions are canceled over a reasonably predictable period of time.

Five of the high judges joined in this ruling; four opposed it. The opposing judges felt that an intangible asset consisting of paid subscribers is the equivalent of goodwill. There was general agreement by all members of the Court that goodwill is the expectation of continued patronage. However, the majority felt that in the Newark case, the customer lists had . . . *an ascertainable value separate and distinct from goodwill.*

Thank the Newark Company

We all should thank the Newark Morning Ledger Company, a newspaper publisher. Its perseverance, painstaking homework, and willingness to put up the litigation costs, were instrumental in moving the granite mountain of IRS bureaucracy a smidgen closer to business-life reality. Small businesses should be especially thankful because they themselves do not have the resources and stamina to undertake such a task. Were it not for the Newark case, Congress would not have added Section 197 to the Internal Revenue Code.

Section 197 is titled: *Amortization of Goodwill and Certain Other Intangibles*. This title alone tells you something about the change of mind of Congress. The phrase "amortization of goodwill" is a totally new concept when selling a business. It means that the seller and buyer can now work closer together to define with specificity each and every intangible encompassed under the umbrella of goodwill. Prior to Section 197 being enacted on August 10, 1993, any attempt to amortize — or cost recover — goodwill was met with disallowance vigor and disdain by the IRS.

The general rule under Section 197 is its subsection (a). This reads in full as follows:

> A *taxpayer **shall be entitled** to an amortization deduction with respect to any amortizable section 197 intangible. The amount of such deduction shall be determined by amortizing the adjusted basis (for purposes of determining gain) of such intangible **ratably over the 15-year period** beginning with the month in which such intangible was acquired.* [Emphasis added.]

Using this new rule, what is the dollar benefit to the Newark Company?

The benefit is a cost recovery in the amount of $4,518,200 per year ($67,773,000 ÷ 15 yrs). This means that instead of tying up $67,773,000 on its balance sheet forever, the company can now get amortization deduction of $4.5 million per year. This is the amount of money that it can make available for other purposes of the business.

The amortization (cost recovery) under Section 197 is a marked change from the past. So much so that we present the "graphics of it" to you in Figure 4.1. On a lesser dollar scale, the same amortization benefits trickle down to small businesses which sell their going concern value along with their more commonplace

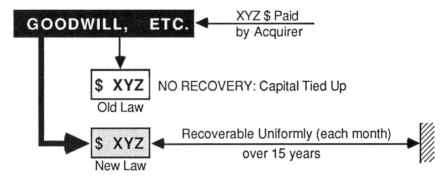

Fig. 4.1 - Old Law:New Law Contrast in Goodwill Cost Recovery

tangible assets. All it requires is good accounting homework and perseverance in sorting out the menu of intangibles that qualify.

"Section 197 Intangible" Defined

What Congress really did was to carve out and define a new category of property that could change hands when a business is sold. This new category is called: *Section 197 Intangible*. It is designated as such in the very opening sentence of the general rule. In the Section 197(a) citation above, recall the phrase: "an amortized deduction with respect to any *amortizable section 197 intangible*."

The above phrase raises two questions, namely:

One.   What is an "amortizable" Section 197 intangible?
Two.   What is a Section 197 intangible?

The implication is that not all Section 197 property is amortizable. So, let's answer the second question first.

Subsection 197(d) defines the term "Section 197 intangible" as meaning any or all of the following:

(1) goodwill;
(2) going-concern value;
(3) workforce in place;
(4) information base;
(5) know-how;
(6) any customer-based intangible;

(7) any supplier-based intangible;
(8) Governmental licenses, permits, etc.;
(9) Covenants not to compete; **and**
(10) Franchises, trademarks, and trade names.

This listing is an all-inclusive checklist of just about everything that constitutes goodwill and "its associated intangibles." Yet, if you will review this listing carefully, and recall some of the items that we discussed in Chapter 3, you will find that two items are missing. The two missing items are patents and copyrights. Because patents and copyrights have ascertainable useful lives, separate from goodwill, they have been a long-time exception to the no-depreciation mandate for goodwill.

"Amortizable" Intangible Defined

Now, let's answer the first question above: What is an *amortizable* Section 197 intangible? Pursuant to subsection 197(c)(1), such an intangible—

means any section 197 intangible—
(A) which is acquired by the taxpayer after the date of enactment of this section [August 10, 1993], *and*
*(B) which is held **in connection with the conduct** of a trade or business or an activity* [engaged in for the production of income]. [Emphasis added.]

In other words, to be amortizable, the goodwill, etc. must be "in connection with" the conduct — sale, merger, and acquisition — of a business. The implication is that the business must continue after the sale. The underlying concept is that there must be a bona fide transfer of ownership of a business, at which time the then itemized and described intangibles become amortizable.

The legislative history of Section 197 reveals that, regardless of the actual useful life of an amortizable Section 197 intangible, the 15-year amortization period applies. That is, neither a shorter period nor a longer period can be used. Furthermore, no other section of the tax code can be used to circumvent this fixed 15-year period, . . . except as expressly provided under specific subsections of Section 197.

Subsections 197(c)(2) and (3) **exclude** from the 15-year amortization rule self-created intangibles and those contrived —

called "churning" — between related parties (through family or business affiliations). In other words, there must be an arm's length change of ownership between a buyer and seller who are neither self-creators nor related to each other. These prohibitions are to avoid self-dealing and any rearrangement of books to take advantage of the 15-year amortization writeoff.

We try to depict in Figure 4.2 the mandatory aspects of Section 197 and its exceptions. In general, the exceptions recognize prior law when not in conflict with new law. After defining immediately below what are the includibles in Section 197, we'll list later the special rules, exclusions, and exceptions.

More Detailed Definitions

The valuation of goodwill and its associated intangibles is extremely important at the time of change of ownership of a business. For this reason, and because of the newness of Section 197, we should define the 10 items above more specifically. For this, we use The House Committee Report (H.R. 2264) prepared by Congress and released on August 4, 1993. Nowhere else in the tax code do these definitions appear. We'll follow the same listing above — (1) through (10) — when defining "Section 197 intangibles."

(1) *Goodwill*. The House Committee Report defines goodwill as the value of a trade or business that is attributable to the expectancy of continued customer patronage. This is so whether the expectancy is due to the name or reputation of a trade or business or to any other factor. It is the "expectancy" factor that characterizes goodwill from other intangibles. This is a primarily a judgment call between buyer and seller.

(2) *Going-concern value*. This is the additional value that attaches to property because it is an integral part of a going concern. It includes the value attributable to the ability of a trade or business to continue to operate and generate sales without interruption in spite of a change of ownership. This is the ongoing "bundling effect" when all tangibles and intangibles are transferred as a package to a new owner.

(3) *Workforce in place*. This includes the composition of a workforce already in place (its experience, education, and training),

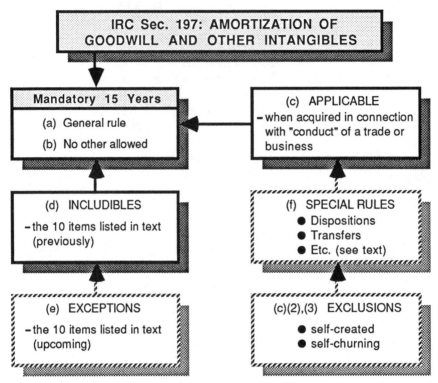

Fig. 4.2 - The Mandatory and Exclusion Aspects of Section 197

as well as the terms and conditions of employment and any other value placed on employees or any of their attributes. The "in place" concept includes all existing contracts with employees, nonemployees (independent contracts) and consultants . . . including any "key employee" contracts.

(4) *Information base.* This intangible includes the cost of acquiring customer lists; subscription lists; insurance expirations; patient or client files; lists of newspaper, magazine, radio, or television advertisers; business books and records; and operating systems. Also included are the value of technical manuals, training manuals or programs, data files, accounting systems, and inventory control systems. Although each of these items may — and should — be valued separately, they are categorized as one intangible only.

(5) *Know-how*. A patent, copyright, formula, process, design, pattern, know-how, format, or similar item is encompassed in the overall concept of a Section 197 intangible. However, special rules apply to patents; computer software; and interests in films, sound recordings, video tapes, book, or other similar property. The "special rules" exclude these items from the definition of Section 197 property, when such items are acquired separately from the existing trade or business [Sec. 197(e)(4)]. Otherwise, know-how includes all of those expertise factors that a new owner needs in order to continue the business uninterrupted.

(6) *Customer-based intangibles*. This intangible refers to the composition of a market, a market share, or any other future provision for goods or services resulting from contractual and other relationships with customers. This intangible is specifically defined to include the deposit base and any similar asset of a financial institution. The term "similar asset" includes checking accounts, savings accounts, escrow accounts, investment accounts, insurance in force, circulation base, and market growth involving relationships with customers in the ordinary course of business.

(7) *Supplier-based intangibles*. This intangible is the value of the future acquisition of goods or services from the suppliers thereof, pursuant to the existence of favorable relationships (contractual or otherwise) with such suppliers. Examples of favorable relations are favorable shelf or display space at a retail outlet, favorable credit terms, favorable supply contracts, or other supplier-based intangibles such as co-op advertising rates, and so on.

All of the above intangibles are treated as inseparable from goodwill. As we'll see later below, all are tax carried as a "vintage account" (all grouped together) amortizable over 15 years. If one or more of the items is disposed of, wastes away, or fails to meet its expectations in less than 15 years, only the tax basis in the vintage account is adjusted. Otherwise, everything stays on the books for 15 years unless the acquired business is resold in less time.

Licenses, Covenants, & Franchises

As was discussed previously in Chapter 3, licenses, covenants, and franchises are separable from goodwill and its associated intangibles. This is because they can be acquired separately from the business, and ordinarily are not created within the business itself. This means that they can be valued separately and, when so valued, can be amortized on a separate 15-year schedule of their own. They are not vintaged together as in the case of the seven intangibles described above.

Let us continue now with more information on licenses, covenants, and franchises. We'll continue with the same sequential numbering as those 10 items listed above comprising Section 197 intangibles.

(8) *Governmental licenses, permits, etc.* Licenses, permits, and other rights granted by a governmental unit, agency, or instrumentality (or renewed by the government) are considered "acquired" for Section 197 purposes. Included are liquor licenses, taxicab medallions, airport landing or takeoff rights, TV and radio licenses, gun dealer licenses, and the like. The fact that the term of a license or permit is renewable, whether for a term certain or indefinite, does not alter its mandatory 15-year amortization period. Excluded from this category of intangibles are government-granted rights to the use of land or the lease of tangible property.

(9) *Covenants not to compete.* If entered into in connection with the direct or indirect acquisition of a trade or business, whether through purchase of its assets, partnership interests, or corporate stock, covenants not to compete are amortizable over 15 years (regardless of the terms of the transaction). Arrangements similar to covenants not to compete, such as compensation or rental paid to the former owner for his continued services or the continued use of his property, are also treated as a Section 197 intangible. Excluded, however, is any additional consideration paid for the covenant which goes into the acquisition cost of common corporate stock.

(10) *Franchises, trademarks, and trade names.* A franchise is defined as an agreement which gives one of the parties to the agreement the right to distribute, sell, or provide goods, services, or facilities within a specified area. Under existing law (Code Sec. 1253(d)(1), a current deduction is allowed for all payments contingent on the productivity, use, or disposition of a franchise, trademark, or trade name. All other amounts, whether

fixed, contingent, or renewal, paid in connection with the agreement are amortizable over 15 years.

By Congress defining licenses, covenants, and franchises as Section 197 intangibles, the intent is that once said items are acquired, they must be amortized over 15 years. This as a mandate will raise potential controversy between the acquirer and the IRS, should the license, covenant, or franchise expire, be rescinded or be disposed of *before* the 15-year period. Fortunately, proposed regulations are construing Section 197 intangibles as consisting of two classes of assets: separables and nonseparables. The "separables" are those which realistically can be shown to have a less than 15-year life.

Overview of Special Rules

Section 197: *Amortization of Goodwill and Certain Other Intangibles*, consists of approximately 3,600 statutory words. These words are arranged in seven separate subsections, namely: 197(a) — General Rule, through 197(g) — Regulations. As to these "Regulations," the IRS has amassed some 25,000 words of regulatory text. Such text should be consulted for clarifying the interpretation of Section 197.

Strictly for overview purposes, we address Section 197(f): *Special Rules*, at this point. Whereas the general rule, subsection (a), consists of approximately 60 words, subsection (f) — special rules, consists of approximately 2,200 words. Thus, obviously, the special rules take up more than half of the new law.

There are nine special rules listed under subsection 197(f). In slightly edited form, these nine special rules are—

(1) Treatment of certain dispositions;
(2) Treatment of certain transfers;
(3) Treatment pursuant to covenants;
(4) Treatment of franchises, etc.;
(5) Treatment of certain reinsurance transactions;
(6) Treatment of certain subleases;
(7) Treatment as depreciation;
(8) Treatment of certain increments in value; and
(9) Anti-churning rules.

Rules (3), (6), (7), and (8) are three lines or less in length each. They are fairly straightforward. The essence of Rule (4):

Franchises, has been covered. Rules (5) and (9) would rarely affect the small business owner.

We will address separately below special rules (1) and (2) only. For small businesses being sold or acquired, these two rules are the most significant. They summarize the overall "sense of Congress" when it enacted Section 197.

For "Partial" Dispositions

Special rule (1) is titled: *Treatment of Certain Dispositions, Etc.* It consists of three subrules, namely:

(A) In general
(B) Covenants not to compete
(C) Controlled groups

A "disposition" is any sale, exchange, abandonment, worthlessness, or other cessation of an identifiable and traceable asset which has been assigned a dollar value when acquired.

The subrule (1)(A) on dispositions reads as follows:

If there is a disposition of any amortizable section 197 intangible acquired in a transaction or series of related transactions (or any such intangible becomes worthless) and one or more other amortizable section 197 intangibles acquired in such transaction or series of related transactions are retained—
*(i) **no loss shall be recognized** by reason of such disposition (or such worthlessness), and*
(ii) appropriate adjustments to the adjusted bases of such retained intangibles shall be made for any loss not recognized under clause (i). [Emphasis added.]

The idea here is that, if a bundle of intangible assets is acquired at one time, or essentially at one time, they are all amortizable simultaneously. During the amortization period, if one or more — but not all — of the intangibles wastes away or disappears, no tax loss is recognized. Instead, the tax basis of the retained intangibles is increased allocably by the amount of unrecovered cost in the disappearing asset(s). We try to depict this concept for you in Figure 4.3. This is the old law concept of vintage depreciating bulk-acquired assets. Thus, for example, an acquirer who purchases a customer list or other data base may not claim a loss deduction as

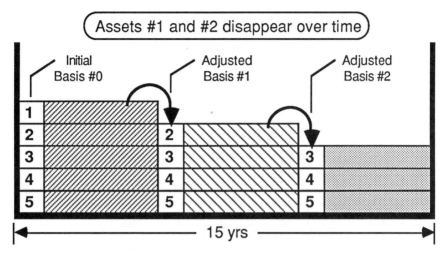

Fig. 4.3 - Readjustment of Basis as Intangibles "Disappear"

customers cancel or terminate subscriptions or services or when a portion of the information in the data base becomes obsolete or worthless.

Subrule (1)(B) stresses the above for covenants not to compete and "similar arrangements." An acquirer may not treat a covenant as disposed of or worthless any earlier than the disposition or worthlessness of the **entire interest** in the trade or business (or substantial portion thereof) with respect to which the covenant was entered into.

Subrule (1)(C) addresses controlled groups and businesses under common control. All members of the same group of controlled *corporations* and all trades or businesses (whether or not incorporated) which are under common control are treated as a single taxpayer for purposes of subrule (1)(A). Thus, one member of a controlled group may not claim a loss when an asset disappears, if another member of the group retains other related intangibles which were acquired at the same time.

When Intangibles Are Exchanged

Special rule (2) is titled: *Treatment of Certain Transfers.* It consists of two subrules, namely:

(A) In general
(B) Transactions covered

For the purposes of this rule, a "transfer" is an exchange of assets (including money) which, under other sections of the tax code, are not recognized for gain or loss purposes. There is an exchange of tax basis only. Any subsequent gain or loss is recognized in downstream time, when there is full disposition of the exchange-acquired items.

The subrule 2(A) reaffirms the exchange concept. It says—

The transferee shall be treated as the transferor when applying this section with respect to so much of the adjusted basis in the hands of the transferee as does not exceed the adjusted basis in the hands of the transferor.

The subrule 2(B) lists the sections of the tax code to which the "transfer of basis" applies, and for which there is nonrecognition of gain or loss. These sections address (1) contributions to corporate capital, (2) transfers between controlled corporations, (3) corporate liquidations, (4) contributions to partnership capital, (5) transfers between affiliated groups, (6) like-kind exchanges, and (7) involuntary conversions.

Let us illustrate the transfer-of-basis rule for Section 197 intangibles. Consider that an acquirer had properly amortized his qualified intangibles over a period of five years. He has 10 years remaining. At this point, his unamortized tax basis is $300,000. He makes a like-kind exchange of the same, or similar, intangibles with another business owner. However, he has to put up an additional $100,000 to make the exchange "fair market equal." The exchange-acquirer's bundle of intangibles now has a tax basis of $400,000. How does he amortize this amount?

Of the $400,000 new tax basis, $300,000 was a "transfer of basis." So, this $300,000 can be amortized over the pretransfer remaining 10 years. The $100,000 has to be amortized over 15 years. This is a split-amortization feature which "falls out" of the transfer-of-basis rule for all subsection 197(f)(2)(B) transfers.

Exclusions from Section 197

The whole focus of Section 197 is on those intangible-type assets that, at time of acquisition, attach to other assets to constitute a trade or business in themselves. If not the entire business, they constitute "a substantial portion thereof." The "acquisition" relates to a change of ownership such as by sale, merger, or other taxable transfers. For example, the acquisition of a franchise, trademark, or trade-name is considered to be an acquisition of a trade or business.

A group of assets (tangible *and* intangible) is considered a trade or business if goodwill or any going concern could *under any circumstances* **attach to** such assets. Hence, the underlying thesis of Section 197 is its focus on those acquisitions which are essential to the continuation of the business after its ownership change. Important in this regard, if applicable, is the continuation of employee relationships or a covenant not to compete. Whether the continuation lasts a few or many years is not a factor.

Apart from Section 197, there are many other kinds of intangibles that are involved in business operation. Unless they are acquired at the time of transfer of controlling ownership, they are excluded from Section 197. Specifically, there are 10 such exclusions enumerated in subsection 197(e): *Exceptions*. (Recall Figure 4.2.) They are—

(1) financial interests in a corporation, partnership, trust, or estate;
(2) interests in certain financial contracts;
(3) interests in land or leases thereof;
(4) certain computer software;
(5) certain separately acquired rights and interests;
(6) interests under existing leases of tangible property;
(7) interests under existing indebtedness;
(8) sports franchises;
(9) residential mortgage servicing rights; and
(10) corporate organization or reorganization costs.

Most of the exclusions above are self-explanatory when you realize that they take place under normal business operations, without there being a change of ownership. For example, interests in land (which are never depreciable or amortizable) are capital assets of their own. Such interests as fee simple, life estate, remainder, easement, mineral rights, water rights, timber rights, grazing rights, riparian (waterfront) rights, air rights, zoning variance, etc. are simply not goodwill-type intangibles.

The exclusion of sports franchises, item (8) above, is an interesting exception. The acquisition of a franchise to engage in a professional sport, plus those items acquired in connection with such acquisition (such as goodwill, going concern value, etc.) do, indeed, constitute a trade or business. However, prior law, namely Section 1056: Player Contracts, addresses in full the taxability of such transfers. As a consequence, sports franchises are automatically excluded from Section 197.

In the above listing of exclusions, we do want to comment further on items (4) and (5). Pending these further comments, we present Figure 4.4 as a summary to understanding the distinction between Section 197 and non-Section 197 intangibles.

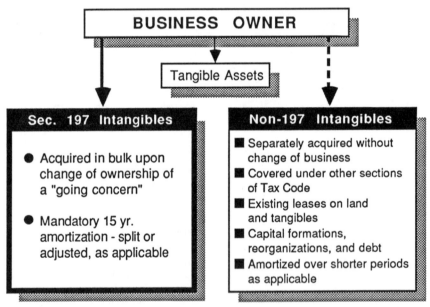

Fig. 4.4 - Distinction between Sec.197 and Non-197 Intangibles

Computer Software

Computer software — item (4) listed above — is "intellectual property" which is readily available for purchase by the general public. As such, it is subject to copyright protection on its own. It is therefore specifically excluded from Section 197. However, the exclusion applies **only if** the software is **not acquired** in a transaction or series of related transactions involving other assets constituting a trade or business.

Subsection 197(e)(3)(B) defines "computer software" as—

any program designed to cause a computer to perform a desired function. Such term shall not include any data base or similar item unless the data base or item is in the public domain and is incidental to the operation of otherwise qualifying computer software.

If acquired apart from the sale or other taxable transaction of any ongoing business, computer software is a tangible asset. As such, it is *depreciated* over five years unless a shorter useful life can be established. Software acquired with a computer as part of its cost (such as when the software cost is not separately stated), is depreciated over the same life as the computer (which is normally five years).

Otherwise, where computer software has been substantially modified to accommodate the user's business, it loses its public domain status. Unless the modifier copyrights his version of the software, or creates an exclusive license for its use by others, it becomes inseparable from the business to which it attaches. Thus, what was previously public domain computer software has been transformed into a Section 197 intangible.

Separately Acquired Interests

Pursuant to subsection 197(e)(4) — listed as item (5) previously — the following interests and rights are excluded from the definition of Section 197 intangibles. That is, they are excluded **if** —

not acquired in a transaction (or series of related transactions) involving the acquisition of assets constituting a trade or business or substantial portion thereof:

(1) an interest in a film, sound recording, video tape, book, or similar property (including the right to broadcast or transmit a live event);

(2) a right to receive tangible property or services under a contract or a right to receive property or services granted by a governmental unit, agency, or instrumentality;

(3) an interest in a patent or copyright; and

(4) to the extent provided in regulations, a right received under a contract (or granted by a governmental unit, agency, or instrumentality) if the right has a fixed duration of less than 15 years or is fixed in amount and would be recoverable under present law under a method similar to the unit-of-production method.

The key to the exception of the above intangible-type items is that they be acquired separately from any sale or acquisition of an entire business (or a substantial portion thereof). Once so acquired, the cost of the rights and interests therein is recovered over the number of units produced, delivered, or sold within the competitive or contractual market cycle.

To illustrate the unit-of-production recovery concept, let us assume that the cost of a separately acquired right is $10,000. The estimated number of units produced, delivered, or sold over a 5-year period is 85,000. In thousands per year, the number of units involved is 35 (1st yr), 20 (2nd yr), 15 (3rd yr), 10 (4th yr), and 5 (5th yr). The cost recovery of the $10,000 over the five years is as follows:

$$1st\ yr\ =\$10,000 \times \frac{35}{85} = \$4,118$$

$$2nd\ yr\ =\ 10,000 \times \frac{20}{85} = \ 2,353$$

$$3rd\ yr\ =\ 10,000 \times \frac{15}{85} = \ 1,765$$

$$4th\ yr\ =\ 10,000 \times \frac{10}{85} = \ 1,176$$

$$5th\ yr\ =\ 10,000 \times \frac{5}{85} = \ \underline{\ \ \ 588}$$
$$\$10,000$$

If, before the end of the five years above, the acquirer's business is sold (in bulk), he has one of two options. He can segregate the particular $10,000 right in the sales contract so that the new owner can pick up where he left off. Or he can allow his

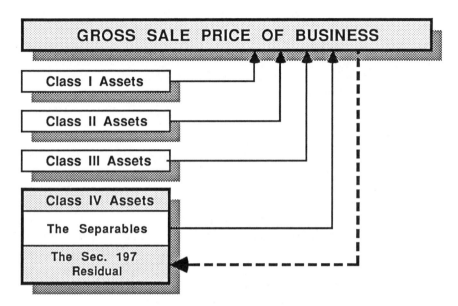

Fig. 4.5 - The "Residual Method" for Valuing Sec. 197 Intangibles

unrecovered cost to be "swept into" the Section 197 intangibles category. Much depends on the relative amount of cost recovery achieved before the business is sold.

New Class IV Assets

One purpose of Section 197 is to augment prior legislation with respect to the valuation of goodwill and its inseparable intangibles. The two prior laws particularly targeted are Sections 338(b) and 1060. Section 338(b) is titled: ***Certain Stock Purchases Treated as Asset Acquisitions: Basis of Assets***. Section 1060 is titled: ***Special Allocation Rules for Certain Asset Acquisitions***. We are going to tell you more — much more — about Sections 338(b) and 1060 in Chapter 7 (for allocating the gross sale price of your business). What we want to call to your attention at this time is that your Section 197 intangibles have to be bulk valued. How and when does one do this?

In principle, valuing your Section 197 intangibles is quite simple. The technique is called the *residual method* of valuation. The "residual" is that amount which is left over after subtracting everything else that you can separately value. The idea is that you start with the agreed gross sale price of your business, whatever amount that might be. Then, you successively subtract Class I assets, then Class II assets, and then Class III assets What is left over — the residual — comprises "Class IV assets." (We'll define these asset classes in Chapter 7.)

In the absence of other definitive clarity, the new Class IV assets comprise all Section 197 intangibles . . . in toto. But, what does "other definitive clarity" mean?

This phrase means that if there are any intangibles which have been separately acquired (and carried on your books as such), or if there is some other provision in the tax code which addresses the treatment of intangibles upon disposition, the value of that item (or those items) can be subtracted off the top of the Class IV residual amount. Then the diminished residual amount automatically becomes the Section 197 value. We portray the simplicity of this concept in Figure 4.5. This is a more sophisticated update of the residual value concept presented back in Figure 3.3 (on page 3-11).

Consider, for example, that your Class IV amount turns out to be $100,000. Of this amount, you can identify and value separately some $62,500 of your intangibles. The net residual amount is $32,500 ($100,000 - 62,500). This residual, then, is the value of your Section 197 intangibles. These intangibles — goodwill and all — cannot be further separated. They must go forward on the books of the new owner as Section 197 property.

In order to arrive at the proper value to ascribe to Section 197 items, you must have sold the business. This means that there is no estimating or valuation technique that you can use beforehand. Though you may have your own ideas as to what these intangibles are worth, you have to silently incorporate said value into the overall pricing formula that you establish for your business. Setting a price for your business is what the next chapter is all about.

5

PRICING YOUR BUSINESS

Pricing Your Business For Sale Is An Exercise In Fair Market Reality. All Of Your Assets — Intangibles As Well As Tangibles — Are "Wrapped Up" And Priced As One. There Are At Least NINE Different Methods Of Evaluation, No One Of Which Is Right-On. A Minimum Of Three Methods Should Be Used (Such As, Adjusted Book Value, Capitalization Of Income, Professional Appraisal) Where The Results Of Each Method Are WEIGHT AVERAGED For Your Initial Listing Price. For Closely-Held Corporations, Book Value And Price-Earnings Value Of The Restricted Stock Also Are Weight Averaged.

Everyone wants to get a fair price when selling his business. But what's a "fair price"? It is elusive at best. The seller wants the highest price he can get; the buyer wants the lowest price. When the deal is consummated, the fair price is the *fair market value.*

The term "fair market value" has been judicially defined as being—

The price which property will bring when it is offered for sale by one who is willing but is not obligated to sell it, and is bought by one who is willing or desires to purchase but is not compelled to do so. [H.H. Marshman, (CA-6) 60-2 USTC ¶ 1284, 279 F 2d 27, Cert. Den., 364 U.S. 918.]

The fair price is whatever a buyer is willing to pay, even if it's the highest price. This was the position taken by the Tax Court in *Cascade Lumber Co.* (DC) 57-2 USTC ¶ 9841, to wit:

*Taxpayer was entitled to a valuation based on the highest price that a **willing and informed buyer** would have paid.* [Emphasis added.]

Other than buyer and seller willingness is whether or not the business is self-sustaining after the sale If there is management continuity, the business is said to be internally self-sustaining. If there is customer continuity, it is externally self-sustaining. Valuing the self-sustaining elements is where all of the "judgment calls" appear.

In this chapter, we want to review the various methods for the overall pricing of your business for sale. No one method gives the "correct" answer. You often have to consider several methods, then "weight average" them for fair pricing. You want the end result — the price you ask — to be reasonable and realistic. You also want it to be a genuine effort that has not been pulled out of the air.

Net Book Value "Plus"

By far the simplest method for setting an overall price on your business is net book value — plus. The "plus" is a multiplying factor which takes into account a compounded rate of return over the years the business has been in existence.

The net book value is all assets carried on the books of the business, less all liabilities therewith. The assets include those intangibles which are carried on the books, if any. For example, if the present seller bought a franchise, a copyright, or the goodwill of a prior owner of the business, he would carry them on his books as capital assets. Like the tangibles he paid for, the intangibles also were paid for. Hence, they are part of his capital investment in the business.

In the case of a partnership or corporation, the net book value can be readily established from the balance sheets on the latest income tax return filed for the entity. The balance sheet information can be updated with current records and pro forma estimates.

In the case of a proprietorship, there is no balance sheet on the tax return. Either construct a balance sheet as per Figure 1.2, or use the depreciation worksheets, ending inventory, and other asset/ liability items reflected in the profit or loss statements.

For example, consider that the owner of a small business can show that his assets totaled $350,000 with liabilities of $125,000. The net book value would obviously be:

Assets	$350,000
Liabilities	<125,000>
Net Book Value	$225,000

Now, suppose the seller has been in business for 12 years. As a solvent business, he figures his rate of return on his investment would have averaged 8% per year. This rate compounded over 12 years comes to 2.518 (check with any accounting or financial handbook). Hence, as a starting point price tag, the business could be worth—

$225,000 x 2.518 = $566,550

Keep in mind that this is a gross figure for initial pricing purposes only. There is no allowance for the business-created intangibles, goodwill, or other self-sustaining factors the business might have. They are all "wrapped up" in the rate of return multiplier above.

Adjusted Book Value

Most solvent businesses are worth quite a bit more than their net book value. This is because, for tax reasons, certain write-offs and adjustments are allowed, such as depreciation, amortization, inventory methods, intangible expenses, losses, and so on. These write-offs, more often than not, produce a lower book value than the actual market value of the assets involved. This is particularly the case for physical plant (real estate) and other capital assets which may well have appreciated in value rather than book depreciated. Also, there is the element of monetary inflation in long-held assets such that replacement costs become a valid consideration.

There are at least six adjustments that can be made responsibly, without giving the effect of "juggling" or "padding" the books. These adjustments related to (1) receivables, (2) inventory, (3) physical plant, (4) equipment, (5) intangibles (carried on the books), and (6) contracts. The idea is to make only those adjustments which are proper in each category — plus or minus — as the case may be. We'll comment on each one of these categories below.

The adjustments to book value affect primarily the asset side of the business balance sheet, and less so on the liability side. Liabilities tend to be fixed with respect to time, unless there are add-ons for late payment, deferred financing costs, or credits allowed on prompt payments. As a solvent business owner, you should take pride in paying your bills within 10 days of submission and claiming the 1% or 2% credits allowed.

Adjustment #1: Receivables — This could be a plus adjustment or a minus adjustment depending on how trade accounts and loans receivable are entered. If they are carried at a discounted value (such as for trade accounts over 90 days and loan accounts over one year), there could be a plus adjustment if collection experience is better than discounted. If the receivables are carried at full face value, a minus adjustment would be in order. Rarely does any business collect 100% of the face value of all of its receivables.

Adjustment #2: Inventory— Because of the various accounting methods allowed for inventory purposes, most businesses choose a method that reports the lowest possible ending inventory. There are income tax reasons for this. The lower the ending inventory, the lower the tax for a given sales volume. Consequently, over a period of years, the ending inventory carried on books (including work in progress, parts, materials, and supplies) is almost always lower than the actual wholesale value of the items on hand. Thus, a plus adjustment is required.

Adjustment #3: Physical Plant — This is primarily real estate: land, buildings, and leasehold improvements. Land is a sterile asset on the books. No amount for depreciation is allowed, yet it tends to appreciate over time. Buildings and leasehold improvements are depreciated for tax purposes, but they also tend to appreciate in market value. Consequently, the physical plant of a business is invariably greater — often, significantly greater — than its book value. This is a plus adjustment indeed.

Adjustment #4: Equipment — Machinery and equipment, including furniture, fixtures, and instruments, all have been depreciated on the books. For this, accelerated depreciation and special elective first-year write-offs are used. As a result, its actual market value as used equipment is greater than its book value. Furthermore, monetary inflation takes its toll when the equipment is replaced. This is a case where replacement cost, rather than market value, is a better yardstick for plus adjustments to book values.

Adjustment #5: Intangibles — Intangible items carried on the books would be franchises, trademarks, patents, copyrights, restricted-issue licenses, and the like. If acquired at time of business startup, these items are generally relatively low in initial value. As a result, they tend to "disappear" off the books over time. Since their values can be computed in terms of the business success (recall Chapter 3), they can cause a rather major plus adjustment to their initial book values.

Adjustment #6: Contracts — Except for security deposits which are carried on the books as current assets, the value of existing contracts tends to get lost in the operating expenses of the business. Yet, these contracts (leases, suppliers, employees, insurance, etc.) are assets which further the going concern value of the business. The expenses for the remaining life of the contracts should be resurrected and assigned a plus adjustment to their book value.

Strictly for illustration purposes, we present in Figure 5.1 a tabulation of how the above adjustments might be made to a small business being offered for sale. Once an adjusted book value is established as illustrated, the result is the asking price tag. There are no further adjustments for return on investment, inflation, goodwill . . . or whatever.

Professional Appraisals

One acceptable way to value a business is to engage a professional appraiser who has valued similar businesses in the past. This person will expect you, the seller, to provide him with all of the basic data and information that he will need to perform his analysis. He will definitely want your tax returns and financial statements for the past five years . . . or for your entire business history if less than five years.

A professional appraiser works on three axioms, among others:

Adjustments to Current Balance Sheet			
ITEM	Book Value	Adjustment	Adjusted Value
Cash	$ 22,000	- 0 -	$ 22,000
Receivables	310,000	< 10,000 >	300,000
Inventory	180,000	80,000	260,000
Physical Plant	350,000	200,000	550,000
Equipment	95,000	25,000	120,000
Intangibles	1,000	60,000	61,000
Contracts	30,000	< 12,000 >	18,000
TOTAL ASSETS	988,000	343,000	1,331,000
LIABILITIES	462,000	30,000	< 492,000 >
	Net Adjusted Value ▶		839,000

Fig. 5.1 - Using Book Value for Pricing a Business

1. He wants to know why you are *really* selling. This influences his interpretation of the data you provide him, and gives him a better insight into judgment calls on his recommended pricings.

2. He understands that sometimes a business may appear to be healthy and profitable on the surface, but may in fact be drowning in red ink below the surface. He does not want to be caught by any surprises that may later jeopardize his professional reputation.

3. While he does not represent the buyer, he is aware that a prudent buyer doesn't take your word or his word for everything. Such a buyer will investigate the tax return data himself, and/or invite his own professional appraiser to the scene.

Most professional appraisers have a checklist of inquiring procedures they go through. Each procedure is intended to bring out the best and the worst in your business. Many will concentrate more heavily on the financial aspects of your business. This is where they get into analysis of your cash flow, debt vs. equity, working capital, source and application of funds, inventory turnover, aging of accounts receivable/payable, verification of cash balances, sales and profit ratios, etc. Professionally appraising a business is a whole field of endeavor in itself. All we can do here is to outline in Figure 5.2 some of the highlights involved.

Area of Review	Scope of Inquiry/Analysis
History of the Business	Founders, owners, name, form, records
Market & Competition	Products, services, sales, literature, "niche"
Sales & Administration	Advertising, distributors, sales, staff, discounts
Manufacturing	Facilities, equipment, process time, safety
Employees / Contractors	Policies, turnover, benefits, attitudes
Business Reputation	Bankers, suppliers, customers, associates
Physical Plant	Location, square footage, owned, leased
Ownership	Total current, age, experience, percentages
Books of Account	Type, location, up-to-dateness, methods
Financial Analysis	Cash flow, accounts aging, profit ratios
Management	Ownership, policies, covenants, controls
Regulatory Matters	Inspections, frequency, zoning, tax returns

Fig. 5.2 - Items That Professional Appraisers Evaluate

One area that appraisers particularly like to work on is your *liquidity ratio*. This is your quick assets (cash plus accounts receivable) divided by your current liabilities.

Appraisers also like to display your *profit margins*, particularly: gross profit margin (gross profit divided by gross sales) and operating profit margin (operating profit divided by gross sales). The "gross profit" is your gross sales less cost of goods and services sold; the "operating profit" is your gross profit less all operating expenses (excluding depreciation and amortization).

After all analysis and presentations of charts and diagrams, a professional appraiser will give his recommendation of a pricing range. Because he is an independent observer, his pricing — although not accepted as gospel — is regarded as having less bias in the seller's favor than if the same pricing range were proposed by the owner(s).

Multiple of Earnings

Another pricing method that can be used is the multiple-of-earnings or capitalization-of-income method. A seller can employ this method himself without recourse to professionals and consultants. He simply takes the last three years of his tax returns, and extracts the pretax net earnings of his business. He uses "pretax" earnings in order to nullify out any aggressive tax accounting techniques he may have used (such as depreciation, amortization, ending inventory accounting, prepaid operating expenses, etc.) to get his taxable income as low as feasible. A buyer may use entirely different techniques for his own tax purposes.

The current year projected (pretax) earnings are also computed by using all current income and expense data. This is the upcoming tax return which is to be prepared, but which is not yet due for filing. The seller then lists this earnings data on a piece of paper as follows: (The figures are illustrative only.)

year 3 —	$ 50,000	(earliest year)
year 2 —	80,000	(intermediate year)
year 1 —	100,000	(latest year)
year 0 —	125,000	(current year, projected)

The seller looks at these figures and asks himself: "To earn this kind of money, what amount of capital would I have to invest, and what rate of return could I expect with alternative investments in today's market?"

Much depends on the business risks involved, and on the general state of the economy and inflation. For low risk businesses and low inflation environment, the rate of return might be 8% or lower. For high risk businesses and high inflationary times, the rate of return might be 15% or higher. It is not that these rates are guaranteed; they are simply "expectations" that any prudent buyer would want to see.

The term "capitalization" is the reciprocal of an expected rate of return. That is, $1 \div 8\% = 12.5$; $1 \div 15\% = 6.67$, for example. These capitalization numbers are the "multipliers" that are used on the net earnings listed above.

Suppose we choose the 6.67 multiplier (15% rate of return). Which years above do we use: year 3, 2, 1, or 0?

Answer: We use them all . . . and *weight average* them. That is, we use year 1 and give it a weighting factor of 50%; it is the most recent and most reliable data we have. Next, we average years 3, 2, and 1, and give that figure a weighting factor of 30%. It is actual data, but it is several years past. We give year 0 (the current projected year) a weighting factor of 20%. Although part of the data is real, the projected portion may be sightly optimistic (because of the pending sale).

The results of our example selections are presented in Figure 5.3. As you can see, the overall pricing figure comes out to be about $650,000. We have tried to weight average the data in what we believe to be a reasonable manner. The result is based on verifiable pretax earnings times an assumed capitalization multiplier.

A 15% Rate of Return Capitalizes at 6.67 [1 ÷ 0.15 = 6.67]					
Text Years	Earnings Data	Earnings Multiplier	Capitalized Amount	Weighting Factor	Weighted Value
[3,2,1] av.	$76,667	6.67	$511,368	30%	$153,410
1	100,000	6.67	667,000	50%	333,500
0	125,000	6.67	833,750	20%	166,750
/////////////			Total Weighted Value ▶		653,660

Fig. 5.3 - Example of Weighting Factors and Income Multipliers

Comparable Business Multipliers

If you have a business that is comparable to other businesses which have been sold — anywhere in the nation — there is a simple and time-saving pricing approach that can be used. This involves the use of the same multipliers that other businesses of your kind have used. This requires that you know, or can gain access to, what these multipliers are. Probably the best way to get this information is to contact a business consultant, and pay him to dig up the information for you. Or, dig it up yourself through financial journals or business and real estate libraries.

For example, suppose you have an accounting, medical, or legal practice that you want to price for sale. Professional associations might have an in-house bulletin board listing service with some advisory limits. But, if not, you have to ask yourself what is the important element of your business that a potential buyer would want. He doesn't want your expertise, because he has his own. He wants your *client base*. More particularly, he wants the transferability of your client base.

Historically, when selling a professional practice, the new owner loses at least 25% of the former clients and, in some cases, as much as 50%. Hence, the multiplier here is less than 1, ranging from a high of 0.75 to a low of about 0.50. It is applied to a weighted average of the last three years of client billings. To this figure, the seller adds the market value of his tangible assets (less liabilities), to arrive at a pricing figure.

Liquor stores, cocktail bars, convenience grocery outlets are bought and sold virtually every week somewhere in the United States. Goodwill is not a factor. The standard pricing formula goes like this: To the value of the inventory, add the market value of all tangibles (less liabilities thereon). Then add the fair market value of the liquor license, entertainment license, or applicable franchise. Then, as a sweetener, add two or three times the historical *monthly* gross sales.

For businesses where customer loyalty is the self-sustaining mainstay — such as insurance agencies, pharmacies, and tax preparation — the typical multiplier is 1 to 1.5 times the historical annual billings of the business. To this amount, there is added the inventory, accounts receivable, and tangible assets (less liabilities) at fair market value. Included in the annual billings multiplier are the customer lists.

For businesses where customer loyalty is fickle — such as advertising agencies, small radio stations, and independent motels — the multiplier is 0.75 to 1 times the most recent annual billings. This includes the name of the business being sold, if the new owner wishes to continue using it. If not, a covenant-not-to-compete may be in order (which is added to the multiplied amount). As with all small businesses, all tangible assets (less liabilities) are added to the multiplier amounts.

There is a common thread running through the multiplier comparables above. The multiplier range is quite low: from about 0.5 to 1.5. It applies to the historical annual gross billings, where "historical" means the general average of the three most recent years. The multiplier amount includes all goodwill and intangibles, except where special items (such as a franchise, license, or copyright) can be valued separately in good faith. Otherwise, all tangible assets (less liabilities) are priced at their market value in good used condition.

Full Replacement Cost

Another way to value a business for sale-pricing purposes is its full replacement cost. You list every asset of your business — the intangibles as well as the tangibles — then set out to replace them at full current cost. Buy new or used, whatever is currently available on the market. It's like going out and buying parts and pieces of the business (including customers and suppliers) and building a duplicate business exactly like the one you now have. You do not need professional appraisers, business consultants, or comparable multipliers to do this. You can do it all by phone, fax, mail, or personal visits as necessary. There is no better way of knowing what your business is worth than trying to replace it all at once.

Replacing your physical plant and tangible assets (including parts, materials, supplies, and inventory) consists of making phone calls and getting bid quotes. Accept the best terms and costs that you can get. If you would have to borrow money to defray these costs, consider the interest on that money as well.

Replacing your intangibles will be more difficult. But not particularly so if you take a 3-step approach. The first step is to focus on those intangibles which can be bought. These are such items as start-up costs, franchises, licenses, permit fees, leases, etc.

The second step involves those intangibles where your personal time and effort (and that of your co-owners) was the motivating factor in their creation. This would involve creating a name and logo, designing your plant, shop, or office layout, establishing management policy, setting up books of account, negotiating contracts, establishing contact with suppliers (and arranging payment terms), compliance with regulatory requirements . . . and so on. Estimate the time and materials that you and your co-owners put into this effort, including fees paid to consultants. Price your time reasonably and total it all.

The third step for replacing your intangibles has to do with your customer or client base. If you are a retail business, advertising is your main source of customer draw. Go back and look at your advertising expenditures for the past three years and total them. It takes at least this long to generate any repeat business. If you are a wholesale business, you have to pay commissions to reps to go out and drum up business for you. Look at your expenditure records for "commissions paid" for the past two years and total them. If you are a service business, you probably have some on-going institutional-type ad running, plus a discount fee of 5% to 10% to new customers referred to you by others. For your most recent year only, to your advertising costs add a 5% or 10% "multiplier" of your total billings.

Total all of the above. The result should be the replacement cost — or nearly so — of your existing business. No prospective buyer is going to pay full replacement cost. He'd prefer, instead, to start his own business from scratch. Nevertheless, reconstructing what your replacement costs would be helps to put a ceiling on the highest possible price that you could ever hope to get.

Closely-Held Stock

A closely-held corporation is a small business entity, organized in corporate form, where five or fewer principals own more than 50% of the voting stock. The stock is "restricted" in that it cannot be publicly traded. It can be sold only to sophisticated buyers and those familiar with corporate operations of a business. Since there is no ready market for the stock, valuing it for pricing purposes becomes a balancing act between net book value and discounted market value estimates.

Upon determining a specific price for the stock, the price of the business as a whole is fixed. It is the unit price per share times the number of shares outstanding. There is no separately valuing of the tangibles and intangibles, then totaling them. The unit share price fixes the price for the entire business, goodwill and all.

Determining the unit share price is a 3-step process. Step 1 is simply the net book value of the business — from the latest *monthly* corporate balance sheets — divided by the number of shares outstanding. This is called the "book value" per share.

For example, consider that there are 100,000 shares outstanding. The latest monthly balance sheet shows the following totals:

Assets	$1,000,000
Liabilities	< 600,000>
Net book value	$ 400,000

Hence, the book value per share is

$$\frac{\$400,000}{100,000 \text{ sh}} = \$4/sh$$

Step 2 requires using the pretax earnings per share, to which a *price-earnings multiplier* is applied. This gives the P/E (price-earnings) value per share. Publicly traded stock is valued this way.

For example, assume that the pretax net earnings of the business (from the latest monthly profit or loss statement) are $100,000. This converts to $1 per share earnings ($100,000 ÷ 100,000 shares). These are real earnings. The trick now is to select a P/E multiple that is reasonably representative of restricted stock. Publicly traded stock ranges from 15 to 30: it all depends on the popularity of the company. Restricted stock P/E's are more like 5 to 15 . . . if this high. Let's assume a multiple of 10. This means that the P/E value of our stock is $10 per share ($1/sh x 10).

Now we have two pricing values: book value ($4/sh) and P/E value ($10/sh). Which one do we use? We use both, but we weight them differently. This is Step 3.

Let's assume that we weight the book value at 40%. We know that book value is the rock bottom figure that we wouldn't even seriously consider. Let's weight the P/E value at 60%. We know there's a market out there to which we can sell. With these assumptions, our price tag would be:

	$/share	Weight %	Weighted Value
Book value	4	40	1.60
P/E value	10	60	6.00
			$7.60/sh

Once we arrive at a unit share price, we can sell 1,000 shares, 10,000 shares, or the whole ball of wax: 100,000 shares. If we sold all the shares, our initial offering price of the entire business would be $760,000 (100,000 sh x $7.60/sh).

Liquidation Value: Cash

There is always one last-resort method of pricing a business, no matter what. This is its liquidation value. You sell everything for spot cash: piecemeal or in bulk, however you can. This approach assumes that you shut down the business, sell its assets, and pay off all liabilities. This produces the absolute bottom dollar for the business. There is no point in selling below this value. It is an all-cash deal.

When selling for cash in liquidation, there is always some discounting to do. For most items, the discounting is done relative to book value. In this case, the liquidating value is less than 100%. For some items, particularly those which have appreciated markedly in value (such as land, buildings, franchises, patents), the discounting is done relative to market value. Typically, the market value of real property exceeds 100% of book value.

Certain capital assets — such as copyrights, franchises, liquor licenses, patents — may sell above book value; however, most depreciable assets will sell at below book value. Such items as work-in-process, leasehold improvements, deferred financing costs, proprietary intangibles, etc. will require deep discounting — below 50% of book value — if they sell at all.

When trying to establish the liquidation value of your business, you have to touch base with real estate agents, used equipment dealers, commercial auction houses, salvage dealers, and others who traffic in bankrupt properties and businesses. You may even have to envision a going-out-of-business (liquidation) sale of your own. There are professional liquidators out there. A few hours' consultation with a reputable liquidator — pay his full fee — will bring pricing reality close to home.

We are not advocating that you actually liquidate your business. After all, if it's a solvent business, why would you do such a thing? But as a *bottom-pricing* method for valuing your business, you certainly should take a look at the liquidation approach.

Several Methods Needed

Since there is no "blue book" for second-hand businesses like there is for used cars, there is no standard reference for seller and buyer to consult for comparative pricings. This means that there is no one way to calculate a business value. Several methods must be used, and the results weighted. We believe that no fewer than three methods should be used.

For summary purposes, we display in Figure 5.4 the various methods presented in this chapter. We also include one that we have not discussed, namely: Discounted projected earnings. This is a *10-year projection* of earnings, using present-value factors, postulated rates of return, and selected capitalization rates that are designed to make the business extremely attractive. It is a speculative pricing technique which is not a viable option, in our opinion.

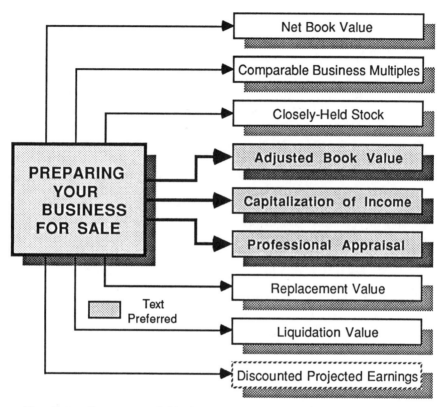

Fig. 5.4 - Summary of Methods for Pricing a Business For Sale

If we had to suggest which three methods, at least, should be used when pricing your business, we would list the following:

Method A — Adjusted Book Value
Method B — Capitalization of Income
Method C — Professional Appraisal

Method A: Adjusted book value, provides a good exercise in self-discipline and analysis by the seller. It "forces" him to review his books of account diligently and to search out those of his assets whose market values are greater than their book values. It also requires that he define his intangibles in terms of their value to a buyer and price them separately, even though not carried on his books. This method is purely introspective and does not involve the use of "comparables" and "multipliers" from other similar businesses. Of the three methods suggested, we feel that Method A is a "must."

Method B: Capitalization of income, also called multiple of earnings, is a form of sophistication that implies greater accuracy than is actually the case. It is more of an exercise in "number crunching" that impresses a lot of business professionals. It requires a religious adherence to pretax earnings for computational basics. It also requires assessment of risks and average rates of return for the industry. These expected rates of return are "capitalized" to become multipliers for weighting posted earnings and current-year projections.

Method C: Professional appraisal, probably has more influence on the buyer than the seller. This is because of the independent status of the chosen appraiser. He'll provide a hefty written report with tables, diagrams, and comparables, lots of financial ratios, and the like. He'll use various hybrid methods of his own to come up with a recommended pricing for the business.

When using three different methods, you are going to get three different results. One solution is to weight each method with your own judgment of their relative reliableness. For example, suppose the results of the methods above are as follows, with the weighting factors shown:

	Value	Weight	Extended
Method A	$150,000	40%	$ 60,000
Method B	250,000	25%	62,500
Method C	200,000	35%	70,000
		100%	$192,500

From this tabulation, the most probable pricing value would be $192,500. It differs from that arrived at by each of the methods separately.

As is evident above, by using three different methods, you get a high value and a low value. This gives you a "framing-in" range. It is then up to you and the buyer to settle on some middle ground.

6

CONSUMMATING THE SALE

A Business Is Not Sold Until All "Terms And Conditions" Are Fulfilled And Verified. Doing So Requires Compromising With Reality. Potential Buyers Need To Be Screened For Seriousness, Expertise, And Financial Means. Afterwards, A Mutual Exchange Of DISCOVERY And DISCLOSURE Is Required. To Protect Each Party Against Misrepresentations Or Misdeeds Of The Other, "Covenants And Warranties" Are Set Forth In A CONTRACT OF SALE. When The Sale Closes, A "Settlement Statement" Is Issued By The Escrow Agency. Before This, However, Formal Instructions To ESCROW Must Be Executed.

Businesses throughout the U.S. are bought and sold every day . . . or nearly so. For both parties, the buy-sell arrangement is often the largest single transaction (dollarwise) in their business careers. For the seller, the sale represents the culmination of years of hard work — and risk. For the buyer, the purchase may be the start of a new business, expansion of an existing one, or the opportunity for increased profits — and risk.

The consummation of the sale usually occurs only after there has been much give and take by both parties. Neither side gets everything that he initially wanted. The buyer winds up paying more than he intended. The seller winds up receiving less than he expected. This is the process called "fair marketing" . . . at arm's length.

The process is not one which can be accomplished in one or two meetings between the principals, nor in several meetings between their intermediaries. There is more to consummating the sale than agreeing to the gross sale price alone. There are consultant and appraisal fees to be paid; there are financial terms to be worked out; there are tax considerations to clarify; there is a detailed listing of assets to be verified; there are regulatory requirements to fulfill; there are legal documents to prepare; and there is a transition from old ownership to new ownership to be thought through.

In this chapter, therefore, we want to bring the constraints of reality into focus. We also want to create an awareness in you that there's a "silent partner" — the IRS — who'll come on the scene after the sale to tell you, by demanding money from you, what you should or should not have done. Consequently, as you consummate the sale, you want to avoid any under-the-table dealings or any other appearance of impropriety. You want the closing deal to be bona fide and recorded in every legal way. By all means, you want an enforceable sales contract where all the terms and conditions are adequately spelled out.

Weigh the Buyer's Needs

Any prospective buyer who has responded to the public offering of your business for sale has the right to ask general questions about your business. He wants to know why you are selling; your business history; your product or service line; etc. Likewise, you have the right to ask questions of the buyer. Why is he interested in buying; what prior business experience does he have; how will he use the business or transform it; what are his expectations and participation in continuation of the business; etc.

In the earliest stages, you want to screen your respondents for those who are serious and have "the ability to pay." Let your agent or broker do most of this screening for you. Do not let bargain hunters, predators, and others that we depict in Figure 6.1 get through.

The purpose of your inquiries is to find out what the buyer's needs are, and how sophisticated he is in business matters. This information gives you a foretaste of those assets for sale which are important and those which are unimportant to the buyer. Expect to make concessions on the unimportant matters, while holding firm to the important items.

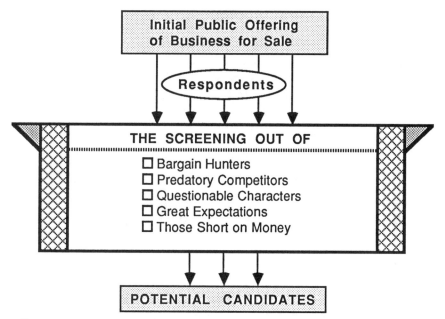

Fig. 6.1 - Screening Out Unwanted Respondents to a Sale Offer

For example, if the likely buyer is to be a first-time business owner, you want to be particularly careful. Because of his lack of experience, he'll want a lot of free consultation and guidance after the sale closes. The risk is high of his accusing you of not disclosing all defects, deadbeats, and slow periods of your business. You want to be on guard for potential post-sale lawsuits. This is the kind of buyer with whom you should not negotiate too much on price and terms.

If a potential buyer is looking to expand his existing business, and your business enhances that expansion, any post-sale consultation and follow-through will be minimal. Experienced business owners have their own management, marketing, and operating style. This means that they don't want you around after the sale.

If a potential buyer wants your real estate, shop facilities, and retail outlets because of your location, any other assets you offer in the package may be meaningless to him. To see how important your location is to the buyer, check with other brokers and business advertisers in your area. Are there other businesses similar to yours being offered for sale? If not, you know that your particular location is important to the buyer. This is where you drive a hard bargain, and concede on peripheral matters.

If a potential buyer wants your product line, your government license, your franchise, or your patent or copyright, he is interested primarily in strengthening his competitive position. He already has his own physical plant in position and operating. So, unless your tangible assets can be separately sold later, the buyer will be uninterested in said items.

If a prospective buyer is a professional person on his own, his primary interest will be in your customer and client base. He'll probably care less about your office equipment, supplies, and staff. Customers who pay on time, who are loyal, and who are repeats, are a joy to behold. This is the gemstone of your business which you don't want to undersell.

Use Advisors Selectively

An agent or broker is your intermediary only. He/she is not your professional advisor on financial, tax, and legal affairs. Your intermediary helps you lure potential buyers, screens them, sees that you make all the proper disclosures, and verifies that recordings have been made in official (public) records when the sale closes. On other matters, you'll need professional advisors at various times between the luring of buyers and the closing of the sale.

Even though you may be widely knowledgeable of the business on your own, it is naive to think that you can avoid entirely the services of financial, tax, and legal advisors. Selling a business is a complex transaction. Unless you have engaged in several sales of businesses the past, there are always some "fine points" that crop up, for which expert advice is needed. This is where qualified professional consultants come in.

Your financial advisor should be a person with credentials in business, finance, and banking. Such a person should be engaged to check the calculations of your asking price, check the calculations of the buyer's offer of price and terms, check on the credit worthiness of the buyer, compute the present worth of the buyer's offer of installment terms, and generally keep you posted on the financial reality of the transaction.

Your tax advisor should be a person who has intimate knowledge of your books of account, your tax returns, employer tax matters, and the tax basis of the assets that you are offering for sale.

He should be engaged to alert you to the tax consequences of each asset in your offering bundle. Request that he make those preliminary tax calculations that are of immediate interest to you. He could also suggest how you might frame certain assets to give tax benefits to the buyer. If you can show the buyer that he is getting some tax benefits out of the deal, you have helped to make a friend out of the buyer instead of an adversary.

Your legal advisor should be a person who is familiar with the business law of your state, and with required notices to regulatory agencies. He should be engaged to review all titles to property, all existing leases and contracts, all product and service liability insurance terms, and any pending litigation outstanding against you. After you and the buyer come to a general agreement as to price and terms, you want your legal advisor to prepare the sales contract: first a draft, then a revision, then the final. The sales contract — when signed by both parties (and notarized) — becomes an enforceable legal instrument confirming the validity and terms of the sale transaction.

Your advisors are just that: advisors. They are not decision makers for you. Call on them frequently and pay them promptly. But keep them in the background. Nothing can stall or kill a deal more than seller and buyer each having his own entourage of advisors present when trying to reach a "meeting of minds." Some advisors can be arrogant and intimidating. Some are not above attacking the personal character and professionalism of the opposite side. If you really want to sell your business and come to agreeable terms with your buyer, keep your advisors out of sight. Insist that the buyer do likewise.

The Full Disclosure Stage

Once you are reasonably satisfied that the buyer is for real, you are ready to enter the stage of making full disclosures. You don't dump all of your books, records, tax returns, contracts, product inventory, depreciation schedules, and customer lists on him all at once. You do it in stages. Treat each stage of disclosure as a separate screening hurdle. If he "passes" the one hurdle, go to the next . . . and to the next. Our proposed sequence in this regard is presented in Figure 6.2.

The idea behind Figure 6.2 is that you want the buyer — if he is truly serious about acquiring your business — to be fully informed of your positives and negatives. You don't want to be accused after

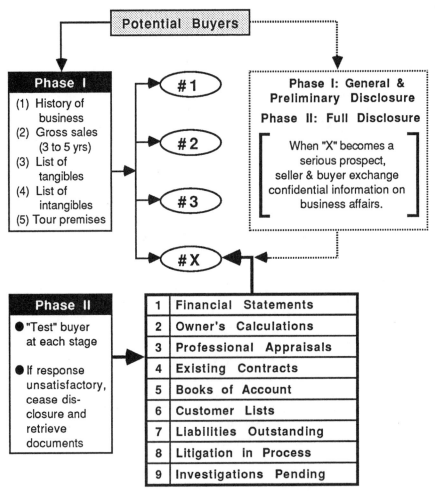

Fig. 6.2 - Sequence of Disclosures to Prospective Serious Buyer

the sale of putting something over on the buyer. You are not trying to defraud him of his money and property. You simply want a fair market exchange. Even so, there'll be some hidden risks on your part . . . and on his part. This is where your advisors and his advisors prove their worth. Both parties want to reduce surprises (and transgressions of confidentiality) as much as possible.

The serious stage of negotiations is functionally one of disclosure and discovery. You disclose what you have and try to discover what the buyer has. The buyer discloses his intent and interests, and tries to discover what post-sale surprises he might run into. This is not the time for give and take on price and terms. It is the time for give and take on *each item* in the bundle of assets that are being sold and acquired. It is the usefulness of each asset in the hands of the buyer that will determine the ultimate pricing and terms. This usefulness will also determine the direction and degree of continuation of the business after the sale.

Agreement on Price & Terms

After all of the shuttling back and forth between principals, brokers, and advisors, there comes put-up or shut-up time. This point arrives when no new information, facts, or questions can be mustered by either side. Either the buyer is serious and wants to buy . . . or not. Either the seller is serious and wants to sell . . . or not. This is the time when a gross sale price has to be settled on.

The publicly listed price of a business when offered for sale is its asking cash price. It is rare indeed for any business to be bought with all cash. Yes, there's some good faith cash down, but mostly it is some percentage of the asking price. The higher the percentage, the more serious the buyer. Consequently, before agreeing to an overall bulk price, there has to be some agreement on the amount of cash down.

You want enough down to cover all of your selling expenses, all of your business debts (unless the buyer is willing to assume them) and those inevitable taxes that you will have to pay on the transaction. At the minimum, when your business is sold, you want to be out from under any residual indebtedness that otherwise might remain. The capital gain and other taxes alone will put you in the 20% plus range. Cash equivalents are acceptable as long as they can be readily converted to cash.

There is no point in discussing other payment terms until the down payment issue is out of the way. When so, you can then consider one or a combination of various payment terms offered. Typically, there are three types of such terms, namely:

1. Installment payments backed up with a secured note.
2. Exchange of property, like and unlike in kind.
3. Issuance of stock and shares in the acquiring entity.

Advising you on payment terms 1 is where your financial consultant may be needed. Advising you on payment terms 2 is where your tax consultant may be needed. Advising you on payment terms 3 is where your legal consultant may be needed.

Offers and Counter Offers

Agreeing on the overall price and terms of a business for sale involves a lot of good old-fashioned horse trading and haggling. One day the deal is on; the next day it is off. And then it is on again. Offers and counter offers go back and forth. Often the brokers on each side are left up in the air. The seller wants some special perks; the buyer wants some special concessions. If both are reasonable persons, ultimately some general agreement will be reached. The payment terms become the final issue of acceptance.

Accepting installment terms (option 1 above) means that you are satisfied with the credit worthiness of the buyer, his history of on-time payments, the available cash flow in the post-sale operation, the type of collateral or security that he puts up, and the market rate of interest that he intends to pay.

Accepting property exchange terms (option 2 above) means that you are satisfied with the appraised values of the like-kind property the buyer is offering (you get a tax deferment here), and that the unlike property is something you can either convert to cash, or hold onto and sell later at a gain.

Accepting stock issuance terms (option 3 above) means that you are willing to take on some of the risks of the acquiring entity, with the expectation of making greater profits later. Keep in mind that you would most likely be receiving restricted or closely-held stock which is not publicly traded. This means that your selling-later options are limited and may not be as lucrative as you were led to believe. This is especially the case if you are issued minority stock where the first rights of refusal are held by the founding principals of the acquiring entity.

Our overall message here is that, before the sale of your business can be really consummated, there has to be some genuine agreement on the overall price and terms. If the terms are too extended in time, say three years or more, there are present-value discounts to consider. A $100,000 payment (in cash, property, or stock) five years from now is only worth about $68,000 in present value (assuming an 8% rate of return). Consequently, because of the terms you accept, you may have to "enhance" the final price to take into account present-value discounting.

Avoid "Aiding and Abetting"

Very few persons in business enjoy the tax burdens that are heavy-handedly imposed on them by the IRS. Because of the magnitude of the money involved — $100,000; $1,000,000; $10,000,000 or so — the tax consequences of selling/acquiring a business cause a major setback to both parties. As a consequence, one of the first true meetings of mind is the desire by both sides to minimize their taxes. This is a natural and healthy affair if it is not carried to extreme.

By carrying to extreme, we mean the various off-the-books arrangements, the intentional overvaluations and undervaluations of assets, and the fictitious credits and allowances shown on the books — all with the intent to distort the bottom line tax results. Under-the-table and confidential deals go on all the time in business transactions. But if the sole purpose is to willfully understate the tax liability of each side, a special tax law comes into play. This is Section 6701 titled: *Penalties for Aiding and Abetting Understatements of Tax Liability.*

In general, Section 6701 imposes a $1,000 penalty on individuals and a $10,000 on corporations for collusion-type activities that produce less tax than the IRS deems proper. The key statutory wording thereof is—

> *Any person who aids or assists in, procures or advises with respect to, the preparation or presentation of any portion of a return, affidavit, claim, or **other document**, who knows (or has reason to believe) that such portion will be **used with any material matter** arising under the internal revenue laws . . . shall pay a penalty with respect to such document.* [Emphasis supplied.]

It is important to note that only one penalty per tax period can be imposed [Sec. 6701(b)(3)]. This means that if several fictitious documents are prepared and used in a given year by a taxpayer, there can be only one penalty: not one for each fictitious document. This helps to save the taxpayer from the obsessional pyramiding of penalties for which the IRS is famous.

Furthermore, it is important to note that the burden of proof when assessing the $1,000 to $10,000 penalty is on the IRS [Sec. 6703(a)]. But this is a weak burden. The IRS does not have to prove actual collusion between the document preparer and the taxpayer. All the IRS has to show is that the document preparer knew — or should have known — that the document (if so used) would produce an understatement of tax liability.

The "should have known" argument is a hackneyed assertion that the IRS always uses when documented information does not produce the highest possible tax revenue. So, be on your guard to avoid the appearance of impropriety in your sale-closing documents.

Typical Documents Involved

In any complex financial transaction, many "papers" go back and forth. There are drafts of offers, preprinted contract forms, preliminary calculations, financial statements, description of assets, etc. For transactional tracking purposes, only certain key documents need to be maintained. Even if the sale doesn't go through as intended, a lot of expenses will be incurred which you'll want to recover on your tax return at some point in time.

Accordingly, the following is a list of documents that you set aside and maintain, as your sale proceeds to its closing:

1. Listing contract with sales agent.
   — this states your initial asking price, the sales commission to be paid, length of time for the listing, and obligations of the agent and seller.

2. Initial advertisement in financial media and with multiple-listing agencies.

3. Professional appraisals made and third-party inventory taken after the initial public offering of the business for sale.

4. Financial statements, books of account, and tax returns disclosed to buyer.

5. Memorandum of offer and acceptance between buyer and seller.

6. Formal sales contract between seller and buyer.

7. Instructions to escrow officer of the title company officiating at the sale closing.

8. Public notices (such as Notice to Creditors, Notice of Bulk Sale, etc.) as required by state law.

9. Final closing statement.
— this is a comprehensive settlement of all funds, property, and indebtedness that go through escrow; the statement is separated into "seller's side" and "buyer's side."

We summarize the above for you in Figure 6.3. You can use the figure as a check-off list for the important items to keep. Otherwise, you may be tempted to "keep everything" . . . just in case. If you do this (keep everything), you'll be thoroughly confused when the time comes to prepare your after-the-sale tax return. Keeping everything leads to cluttery recordkeeping and disorganization.

SALE OF BUSINESS: A to Z Signs Galore			
No.	Description	√	pages
1	Listing contract with sales agent		
2	Advertisement: initial public offering		
3	Professional appraisals & computations		
4	Financial statements & tax returns		
5	Memorandum of intent to purchase		
6	The CONTRACT OF SALE		
7	Instructions to escrow agent		
8	Public notices required by state law		
9	Final closing statement (by escrow agent)		

Fig. 6.3 - Key Documents To Be Retained for Tax Purposes

The "Memorandum" Document

Each brokerage firm handling a business sale has its own in-house forms for writing up offers, counter offers, and acceptances of the general terms of the sale. These often are preprinted forms with ample blank spaces for hand entries. When the hand entries become too numerous, some agents will type up their own Memorandum of Intent (offer and acceptance) and try to get both parties to sign the same document. The idea is to put something in writing that both sides can consider.

Although the memorandum of offer may be prepared by either the seller's agent or the buyer's agent, technically the offer is made by the buyer. He is the one who puts up "earnest money" to test the willingness of the seller to sell. The amount of earnest money — typically between $1,000 and $10,000 — is a good faith token only. It has no relationship to the percentage of cash down that both sides may have kicked around. If the offer is accepted, the earnest money is credited towards the down payment. If the offer is refused or is allowed to lapse, the earnest money is returned to the offerer.

Because of the tentative nature and generality of the offer and acceptance document, we prefer to refer to it as a *memorandum*. It is more of a statement of intent than a formal sales contract. Its purpose is to encourage a "meeting of minds" rather than getting bogged down in the fine points of transactional details. It leaves open the opportunity to work out the details later.

No offer to buy — nor offer to sell — can stand open forever. The buyer wants to know rather promptly whether the seller accepts or not . . . and vice versa. It is only when and after the memorandum is accepted and *signed* by both parties that it becomes a document for retention.

From an after-the-sale tax point of view, the memorandum document becomes evidence of good faith, economic substance, and profit motive. This kind of documentation is needed should the IRS ever assert that the transaction was a sham. It could make this assertion if it were a below-market-value sale, or if related taxpayers were involved, or if corporate self-dealing were involved, or if there were gross overvaluations that materially tax benefited the acquirer.

Content of Sales Contract

The ultimate goal of "all of the above" is to come to a formal (legal) agreement called: *Contract of Sale, Sales Contract, Bill of Sale,* or *Sales Agreement.* This document is a wrap-up of all the negotiations, representations, and intentions of the parties. In its preamble, it summarizes: (1) the name and address of the business being sold, (2) the name and address of the seller, (3) the name and address of the buyer, (4) the date that the agreement is entered into, and (5) the date when the transfer of possession of all property (subsequently described) is to be completed (called: *closing*).

The WHEREAS preamble is followed by a bold subheading which reads:

IT IS AGREED AS FOLLOWS

Each item of the agreement is separately paragraphed and numbered (**1, 2, 3,** etc.) and subparagraphed (**a**), (**b**), (**c**), etc.) as appropriate. Depending on the extensiveness of the assets being transferred and the conditions precedent to closing, the contract document comprises some five to 15 pages of printed text, with sequential paragraph numberings ranging from 15 to 50.

For example, the very first paragraph is almost always cited as—

1. Sale of Business. The Seller shall sell and the Buyer shall buy, free from all liabilities and encumbrances except as hereinafter provided, the property and business owned and conducted by the Seller under the trade name of_____, at the premises known as_____, including the goodwill as a going concern, the title or lease to such premises, stock in trade, furniture, fixtures, machinery, equipment, and supplies, all of which are more specifically enumerated in Exhibit A as to tangible assets, and in Exhibit B as to intangible assets, attached hereto and incorporated by reference.

Specific separate listings of the assets being sold become important checklists to the seller as protection against claims by the buyer that not all assets have been transferred. The checklists are also important to the buyer for recourse against the seller should there be shortages or defects in title.

We also think there should be an Exhibit C attached to the contract which allocates the purchase price to specific items in Exhibits A and B. This allocation exhibit will come in handy when both seller and buyer prepare their tax returns after the sale. We'll discuss this allocation matter fully in the next chapter.

The contracts of sale differ substantially in formality and length, depending on the form and multiplicity of ownership of the business being sold (proprietorship, partnership, or corporation). Nevertheless, all contracts of sale include such paragraphic items as:

- Purchase price
- Method of payment
- Adjustments to payment
- Contracts and liabilities
- Transfer of licenses
- Taxes and expenses
- Seller's warranties

- Seller's obligations
- Buyer's warranties
- Covenant not to compete
- Risk of loss (pending closing)
- Conditions precedent to closing
- Arbitration of disputes
- ... and other matters

The very last paragraph is usually a statement concerning arbitration procedures, should disputes arise after the contract is signed.

Whatever the total number of paragraphs in the document, the contract ends with the personal or agency signatures of the buyer(s) and seller(s). The signatures are witnessed or notarized in accordance with the local legal practices. A typical such signature block appears as—

IN WITNESS WHEREOF, the parties to this agreement have executed it on _____ (date) _____.

SELLER	*BUYER*
_____/s/_____	_____/s/_____
_____/s/_____	_____/s/_____

WITNESS MY HAND AND OFFICIAL SEAL

Official Seal

_____
Notary Public

A signed and witnessed Contract of Sale is the focal document of importance for financial, tax, and legal purposes. So much so that we present a depiction of its focal role in Figure 6.4. Note that immediately preceding the contract is the Memorandum of Intent (to purchase) and immediately following the contract is Instructions to Escrow (for closing). Also note that we have highlighted a particular portion of the contract designated as: Covenants and Warranties. These are the "make or break" conditions of fulfillment

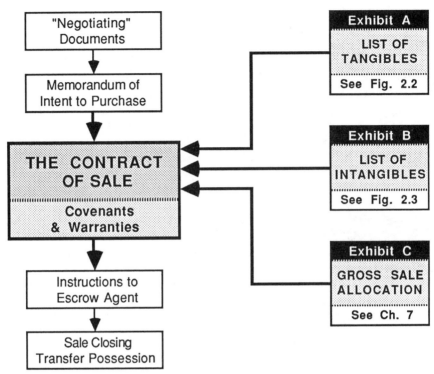

Fig. 6.4 - Focal Role of "The Contract" for Closing a Sale

that precede the final legal closing of the sale. We want to expand on these conditions.

Covenants and Warranties

During the course of negotiations leading up to the Contract of Sale, both parties have made representations to each other, and have exchanged documents, financial data, tax records, appraisals, calculations, and other information. Consequently, at the time of signing the contract, each party wants protection against any misrepresentation or misdeeds of the other. This is where the *covenants and warranties* paragraphs come in. (A "covenant" is a promise to do or keep from doing a specific act; a "warranty" is a guarantee or assurance that the property or item is or shall be as represented.)

There are two sides to the covenants and warranties issue: the seller's side and the buyer's side. There is also a transitional period of time (between signing the contract and the completion of the transfer of assets) during which both buyer and seller assume certain obligations and liabilities.

Typically, the seller covenants and warrants to the buyer that:

(1)   He is the owner of and has good and marketable title to all of the assets described in the exhibits.

(2)   The assets are free of all debts and encumbrances except for those assumed by the buyer.

(3)   The statements made concerning the status and condition of assets, facilities, licenses, contracts, etc. are true and accurate and that *no material fact has been withheld.*

(4)   All financial, appraisal, and tax information furnished to the buyer was prepared in accordance with generally accepted accounting practices.

(5)   No litigation, governmental proceeding, or other investigation, except as disclosed, is pending against said business.

(6)   He will pay all liabilities not assumed by the buyer and will hold the buyer harmless from any claims and liabilities not assumed by the buyer.

(7)   He assumes all risk of destruction, loss, or damage due to fire or other casualty up to the date of closing.

(8)   He will conduct the business up to the date of closing in a regular and normal manner to preserve the goodwill of customers, suppliers, and others having business relations with the business.

(9)   He will give the buyer or his representative during normal business hours full access to the premises, records, properties, and documents as the buyer may reasonably request.

Typically, the buyer covenants and warrants to the seller that:

(1)   The seller shall retain as his property all cash on hand and other incidental items as agreed to, as of the day before the date of transfer of possession or closing.

(2)   The money, note, mortgage, property, or stock (as applicable) required of the buyer shall be delivered on or before date of closing.

(3)   He will process with due diligence all open purchase orders and and all accounts receivable as of the date of transfer and closing.

(4)   He will honor all contracts, insurance, and liabilities that the buyer assumes at time of closing, and shall indemnify seller against any liability or expense arising out of any breach of such contracts occurring after the closing.

(5)   He will perfect all titles of transferred property, including applicable licenses, permits, and inspections, on or before the date of closing.

(6)   He has no knowledge of undisclosed encumbrances, litigation, or other developments that would be materially adverse to the business and its property upon transfer of possession to the buyer.

Alongside of these covenants and warranties, there are (usually) checkboxes or lined spaces where the seller and buyer separately hand initial. This gives each party some assurance that the other side is aware of his/her/its duties and obligations under the Contract of Sale.

Instructions to Escrow

The sale is not complete until the process of escrow is complete. This process is the conveyance of the Contract of Sale to a third party where it is held until **all** of its conditions are fulfilled. The "third party" is a title company or escrow attorney, called: *Escrow Agent*. When the contractual conditions are met, title to all designated property and assets passes from the seller to the buyer. This is called: *transfer possession or closing of escrow.* Thereafter, the buyer is the owner; he assumes all obligations and liabilities from that point on.

To put the closing process into operation, both parties must sign the same set of instructions to the escrow agent. Each escrow agency has its own preprinted 3- to 5-page legal form for this purposes. Typically, the instructions direct the escrow agent to do the following:

1. Hold the Contract of Sale in escrow until closing date.
2. Prepare and record Notice of Bulk Sale.
3. Publish Notice to Creditors in local newspaper.

4. Notify state sales tax, state employment tax, and county property tax agencies.
5. Notify applicable licensing and regulatory agencies.
6. Independently verify all property and assets (including titles, deeds, registrations) to be transferred.
7. Collect and hold all monies, notes, mortgages, stock, and other collateral required for the transaction.
8. Require prompt payment or make other provisions by seller or buyer for creditor claims and debts.
9. Require prompt payment by seller and buyer of all fees and charges incurred during the process of closing.
10. Hold all cash proceeds in an insured interest-bearing account; credit the interest earned to the appropriate parties.
11. Establish procedures for addressing defaults, disagreements, and cancellations by the parties.
12. Obtain the "certified correct" federal tax identifying number of both parties so that, when the transaction is complete, the IRS can be notified.

Both parties sign the instructions, after initialling separate provisions which hold the escrow agent harmless for those matters which are beyond his control. Similar hold harmless clauses apply when the seller or buyer fails to do what each is supposed to do. There are provisions for penalties, refunds, and accounting should — due to no fault of the escrow agent — the sale not materialize.

7

BULK NOTICE & ALLOCATION

Creditors, Including Local Tax And Regulatory Agencies, Are Notified Before Closing Of Escrow; The IRS Is Notified Afterwards. Form 1099-S Highlights The Total Sale Price (Gross Proceeds) Which Has To Be Allocated Among All Assets Transferred. Because Of Different Interests Among Buyer, Seller, And The IRS, "Whipsaw" Tax Positions Occur. To Neutralize These, Section 1060 Requires That CONSIST-ENT ALLOCATIONS Be Set Forth In A Written Document Signed By Both Parties. To Enforce The Allocations, Form 8594 Is A Required Attachment To Each Party's Tax Return.

When a contract of sale has been consummated between buyer and seller, and the matter is in escrow, certain public notices have to be made. These notices are to comply with state law requirements. Foremost in this regard is the statute known as: *Uniform Commercial Code — Bulk Transfers.* The purpose of this body of law is that adequate notice be given to creditors and others (tax, licensing, and regulatory agencies) that the bulk sale of a business is about to take place. Typically, at least 30 days' public notice is required.

To make sure that the bulk sale is also income tax reported, the closing escrow agent must file with the IRS Form 1099-S: *Proceeds from Real Estate Transactions.* This form, or an acceptable substitute, is required even though the business itself may own no real estate.

In addition to the bulk sale notice, the IRS now requires that both buyer and seller mutually prepare a **Form 8594**: *Asset Acquisition Statement*. The purpose of this form is to allocate equitably the final sale price among all of the separately identified assets that were transferred from seller to buyer. There are special tax reasons for this allocation process. The reasons become more self-evident after the sale, at tax return filing time.

In this chapter, therefore, we want to bring all three of the above items into focus, and emphasize how and why they are important to tax return preparation following the sale. Without this foreknowledge, it is too easy to get bogged down in the mass of papers associated with selling a business. The core of this chapter is that Form 8594, with its allocation attachments, becomes the key document for easier tax treatment after the sale.

Purpose of State Law

Many states have bulk sales laws of varying types and coverage. Their purpose is to deal with common forms of commercial fraud. The two most common types are:

(a) The merchant, owing debts, sells out his stock in trade to a friend for less than its worth, pays his creditors less than he owes them, and hopes to come back in the business some time in the future.

(b) The merchant, owing debts, sells out his entire business: machinery, equipment, supplies, and inventory, to anyone for any price, pockets the proceeds, and disappears, leaving his creditors unpaid.

The idea behind the bulk sales laws is to give all creditors advance public notice that a particular business is being sold. Having such notice, the creditors can make their claims to the escrow agent or they can take steps to impound the proceeds of the sale, if necessary. This gives the creditors some degree of protection, provided they act within a 10- to 30-day period of time. However, some buyers object to this delay and regard the state laws as a forced impediment to an otherwise honest transaction.

To guard against undue closing delays, some state laws require that the seller provide the buyer with a complete list of the seller's creditors. The list gives the names, business addresses, amounts owed, and amounts disputed. The list must be signed and sworn to or affirmed by the seller. The buyer then has recourse against the seller for as long as six months after the sale, in the event that the buyer has to pay off any creditors of the seller. In other states, the buyer can assume all or certain debts of the creditor. If he does so, the purchase price of the acquired business can be reduced correspondingly. The buyer then has to give public notice of his assumption within 30 days after the sale.

Most states prescribe their bulk sales laws in their *Commercial Code*. In said code, there is a division titled: *Bulk Transfers*. The term "bulk" means more than half of the entire assets of the seller's business. The term "transfer" means a sale which is not in the ordinary course of the seller's business. These definitions intentionally eliminate the everyday types of sales of merchandise and services.

Effect of No Notice

In California, for example, the law on bulk transfers is found in Sections 6101 through 6111 of its Commercial Code. The essence of California law is that the sale of a business is presumptively fraudulent if no advance public notice is given. A fraudulent transaction is treated as null and void against any *presale creditors* (including tax and regulatory agencies). This does not mean that the sale is null and void with respect to the buyer, if he is willing to go through with the transaction irrespective of the public notice requirement.

To be more specific on the effect of no public notice to creditors, let us cite Section 6105 of the California Commercial Code. This section: Notice to Creditors, says:

> *Any bulk transfer subject to this division except one made by auction sale is fraudulent and void against any creditor of the transferor* [seller] *unless the transferee* [buyer] *gives notice of the transfer in the manner and within the time hereinafter provided.* [Emphasis added.]

Note that the burden of giving notice is on the buyer: not the seller. The rationale for this is to make the buyer liable for any unpaid debts of the seller if no advance notice is given. The phrase "within the time hereinafter provided" means that the notice shall be given at least 10 days before the buyer takes possession of the goods or property.

A transfer in violation of the bulk sales law is not actually void; it is only "voidable." This is so that any creditors of the *buyer* can levy upon the goods or property irrespective of whether or when creditors of the seller come forward. If there are no dissatisfied creditors on either side of the transaction, the bulk sales laws are moot.

Contents of the Notice

Most escrow agencies handling a bulk sale will insist that a public notice of the sale be given. They will do this irrespective of assurances by seller and buyer that there are no dissatisfied or undisclosed creditors in the woodworks. The reason behind this insistence is that there are other state laws which hold the escrow agency liable for any failure to exercise due diligence, especially with respect to tax and regulatory matters. Consequently, as part of its "standard procedure," the escrow agency will publish and record a *Notice of Bulk Sale*. Preprinted legal forms are used for this purpose, headed: *To Whom It May Concern*.

The contents of the notice are spelled out in each state's bulk transfer laws. Using California as an example, the contents are set forth in Section 6107 of its commercial code. That Section says—

The notice to creditors shall state:
(a) That a bulk transfer is about to be made; and
(b) The names and business addresses of the transferor [seller] *and transferee* [buyer], *and all other business names and addresses used by the transferor within three years last past so far as is known to the transferee; and*
(c) The location and general description of the property to be transferred; and
(d) The place, and the date on or after which, the bulk transfer is to be consummated.

Other state law provisions require that the notice be published at least once in a newspaper of general circulation where the property is located, and that it (the notice) be officially recorded in county records at least 10 days before the bulk sale closes.

The notice provides opportunity for all creditors to come forward and file their claims with the escrow agent, if they are not satisfied with prior arrangements that may have been made. Closing of the sale may then be held up pending resolution of these claims.

Separate Notice to IRS

The IRS cannot assess a tax — on income or otherwise — until *after* a transaction takes place. Consequently, it does not need to be notified in advance of the sale of your business. But, once the sale is closed, the IRS gets a prompt reporting on the amount of **gross proceeds** that transpired between the seller (transferor) and buyer. The report or notice — called an "information return" — is made to the IRS by the escrow agency or other person or entity acting as a broker for the transaction.

This gross proceeds reporting to the IRS is a mandatory requirement. It is so prescribed by IR Code Section 6045: *Returns of Brokers*. The general rule thereon, subsection 6045(a), reads as:

Every person doing business as a broker shall, when required by the [IRS], make a return, in accordance with such regulations as the [IRS] may prescribe, showing the name and address of each customer, with such details regarding gross proceeds and such other information as the [IRS] may by forms or regulations require, with respect to such business.

Subsection 6045(c)(1) defines a "broker" as—

any person who (for a consideration) regularly acts as a middleman with respect to property or services.

This clearly includes an escrow agent, title company, real estate broker, attorney, or similar person.

Subsection 6045(e)(2) goes further by defining a "real estate reporting person" as—

(A)   the person (including an attorney or title company) responsible for closing the transaction,
(B)   the mortgage lender,
(C)   the seller's broker,
(D)   the buyer's broker, or
(E)   such other person designated in regulations.

Any person treated as a real estate reporting person . . . shall be treated as a broker for purposes of subsection (c)(1) [cited above].

Subsection 6045(e) itself is titled: **Return Required in the Case of Real Estate Transactions.** This raises the question: Is the sale of a business treated as a real estate transaction if there is no real estate changing hands in the transaction? What do the regulations say on this point?

Reportable Real Estate?

The applicable regulation to the question above is Regulation 1.6045-4 and its subregulations. This regulation is titled: *Information reporting on real estate transactions with dates of closing on or after January 1, 1991.* In general terms, this regulation requires reporting to the IRS any transaction which—

consists in whole or in part of the sale or exchange of "reportable real estate."

Subregulation 1.6045-4(b)(2) goes on to define "reportable real estate" as—

*any present or future **ownership interest** in—*

*(i)   Land (whether improved or unimproved) including air space; **or***
(ii) Any inherently permanent structure, including any residential, commercial, or industrial building.

*. . . the term "ownership interest" includes **any previously created rights to possession or use** for all or a portion of any particular year (i.e., a leasehold, easement, or "timeshare").* [Emphasis added.]

Can you imagine any business for profit being conducted on premises where there are no "rights to possession or use" of land or a building?

Yes, there is ambiguity in the above in that the bulk transfer of a business is not specifically mentioned. But it is not specifically excluded either. The only statutory exceptions are surface/

subsurface crops and natural resources, burial plots or vaults, and temporary mobile structures when—

> *unrelated to the sale or exchange of reportable real estate* [Reg. 1.6045-4(c)(2)].

Your own experience with the IRS should have taught you that whenever there is an apparent ambiguity in tax law, the IRS will always interpret against a taxpayer. We presented a good example of this back in Chapter 4: The Newark Morning Ledger case. That taxpayer had to go all the way to the U.S. Supreme Court to resolve a tax ambiguity.

You are going to report the sale of your business on your own tax return, aren't you? So, why not urge the closing broker to report it to the IRS before you file your return?

Must Use Form 1099-S

The applicable form for broker reporting of a bulk sale to the IRS is Form 1099-S. We suppose that the "S" could be interpreted as to signify "S"ale of a business. Actually, the official title of the form is: ***Proceeds from Real Estate Transactions*** . Note that the word "proceeds" is used. When you look at the form itself — as edited in Figure 7.1 — there is a box with a $-sign for the entry of **Gross proceeds**. As you'll see in a moment, this is the maximum possible amount that can be attributed to the transaction!

The instructions to Form 1099-S define "gross proceeds" as—

> *Any cash received or to be received . . . by or on behalf of the transferor, including the stated principal amount of a note payable to or for the benefit of the transferor. If the transferee assumes a liability of the transferor or takes the property subject to a liability, such liability is treated as cash and is includible as part of gross proceeds. For a contingent payment transaction, include the maximum determinable proceeds. . . . The maximum determinable proceeds means **the greatest amount of gross proceeds possible** if all the contingencies are satisfied. . . . Do not reduce gross proceeds by any expenses paid by the transferor, such as sales commissions, deed preparation, advertising, and legal expenses.* [Emphasis added.]

Form 1099-S Year	FILER's Name, Address, & Zip	Date of closing _____ $ Gross proceeds _____	PROCEEDS FROM REAL ESTATE TRANSACTIONS
FILER's I.D.	TRANSFEROR's I.D.	Legal description of property sold	
TRANSFEROR's Name, Address & Zip			
Copy A - To IRS Copy B - To Transferor Copy C - To Filer		Check if NONCASH is part of consideration paid ▶ ☐	
		Buyer's part of real estate tax $_____	

Fig. 7.1 - Contents of Form 1099-S for Proceeds Reporting

Form 1099-S is prepared in three copies. Copy A goes to the IRS, Copy B goes to the transferor, and Copy C is retained by the filer: the real estate reporting person. Instructions tell the filer to obtain the transferor's "Tax Identification Number" (TIN) by having him certify its correctness "Under penalties of perjury."

If there are two or more transferors, such as when there are two or more co-owners when the business is sold, the gross proceeds can be reported under one owner's TIN, or the gross proceeds can be allocated proportionally to each owner's interest in the business. If the latter is done, a separate Form 1099-S for each owner's TIN is required. The Form 1099-S may be filed with the IRS and a copy given to the transferor, at any time after the closing date, but in no case later than January 31 of the year following the year of sale. In most cases, the reporting broker prepares Form(s) 1099-S simultaneously with his preparation of the required Settlement Statement immediately following the closing.

The buyer (transferee) is unaffected by Form 1099-S. Only the seller (transferor) is affected. You can confirm this in Figure 7.1 by noting that only two persons are shown: transferor and filer. The filer is the reporting broker. Other than reporting the gross proceeds, he, too, is unaffected. The whole idea of Form 1099-S is to tell the IRS's computer what the gross proceeds were. Further note in Figure 7.1 that if any *noncash* goes to the seller, that fact is also reported to the IRS.

Why "Gross Proceeds"?

Why does the IRS place so much emphasis on brokers reporting the maximum possible gross proceeds amount?

There are three reasons, actually.

First and foremost is that, by reporting the gross proceeds, the IRS gets the opportunity to extract "top dollar" (maximum revenue) from an unsuspecting seller. If the seller is overly preoccupied with other business matters, and forgets to report the bulk sale on his income tax return, the IRS waits in the woodwork to nab him. It usually waits from 18 to 36 months after the due date of the seller's return (for the year of the sale). If the seller fails altogether to report the sale, the IRS will assess the maximum conceivable tax on the gross proceeds as though that amount were 100% net profit. And, naturally it adds all the penalties and interest that it can think of. It is a brutal affair. It is all done automatically by computer. A $100,000 sales transaction could easily cause the negligent seller to be confronted with a $65,000 tax bill. Think of what the shock would be if there were a $1,000,000 bulk sale not included on a seller's return?

The second reason is that, by reporting gross proceeds, the seller is put on the spot to report that exact same amount somewhere on his return. The "somewhere" has to be where the IRS's Big Computer can find it and match it. Once the computer matching is done, the seller is on his own to reconcile that amount with other items previously reported on his return. These "other items" are those for which he can recover his *cost or other basis, plus improvements and expenses of sale.* If he does this properly, he will wind up paying less tax than on 100% of the gross proceeds.

The third reason the IRS requires a broker to report gross proceeds is so that the seller will **allocate** the total sale price among all assets that he has transferred to the buyer. This takes us back to Exhibit C in Figure 6.4 (on page 6-15). By allocating properly, the seller can take advantage of different tax forms and their different cost recovery and offset rules, which can further reduce the income tax on the gross proceeds. Hopefully, he initiated the allocation process — with the consent of the buyer — at the time he signed the final version of the sales contract.

In case you are unaware, the term "gross proceeds" is the same as *gross sale price* or *total sale price* . . . whichever terminology you prefer. It is the total agreed selling price of the business, unreduced by any selling or other expenses you may have incurred.

The Allocation Process

For years — since 1955 actually — the IRS has held to the position that, when a going business is sold, the selling price must be allocated among all assets sold. Furthermore, the allocation must be according to the respective relative market value of each asset. The allocable "relative value" is determined from the ratio of the value of each individual asset to the sum total of the value of all assets sold. [Rev. Rul. 55-79, 1955-1 CB 370.]

Be mindful that the relative value of an asset is determined from its market value: not from the gross selling price of the business. This makes sense. Market values can be determined **independently** of the sale, as we tried to encourage you to do back in Chapter 2: Getting Down to Details. It should have been evident in Chapters 5 and 6 that the contractually agreed selling price is a negotiated give-and-take affair for the whole bundle of assets. During the "heat of negotiation," it is impossible to segregate the relative value of each asset in a realistic manner. Hence, the market value approach is used.

Suppose, for example, that the market value of Asset Z has been independently determined to be $62,500. At the same time, the total market value of all assets in the business for sale comes to $500,000. What is the relative value of Asset Z? Suppose the total selling price of the business were $365,000.

Answer: $45,625. First, the *relative fraction* of Asset Z to the total market value ($500,000) of all assets is:

$62,500 ÷ $500,000 = 0.125 or 12.5%

Applying this fraction to the $365,000 sale price, the relative value of Z becomes:

$365,000 x 0.125 = $45,625

If, instead of $365,000, the sale price of the business were $750,000, the allocable value of Asset Z would be $93,750 ($750,000 x 0.125). Thus, as you can see, the allocation process is independent of the actual sale price.

To put the above in perspective, we present in Figure 7.2 a hypothetical allocation example of seven selected asset categories sold in bulk. The items chosen are all tangible assets. Tangible assets are always easier to market value than intangible assets. This

Description of Asset	Column 1 Market Value	Column 2 Fraction of Total Market Value	Column 3 Allocation Value
1. Land	150,000	150/500 = 0.3000	109,500
2. Building	134,000	134/500 = 0.2680	97,820
3. Machinery	112,000	112/500 = 0.2240	81,760
4. Equipment *	62,500	62.5/500 = 0.1250	45,625
5. Vehicles	21,500	21.5/500 = 0.0430	15,695
6. Fixtures	15,000	15/500 = 0.0300	10,950
7. Supplies	5,000	5/500 = 0.0100	3,650
TOTALS	$500,000	500/500 = 1.0000	365,000
* Asset Z in text	Total Sale Price ⟶ Total Market Value		

Fig. 7.2 - Illustration of "The Allocation Process" for Tangibles

is why, back in Figure 6.4, we separated Exhibit A (for tangibles) from Exhibit B (for intangibles).

Once the relative fraction of each asset in the total package is established (Column 2 in Figure 7.2), the same fraction can be applied to other items that go on the seller's tax return. For example, suppose his total selling expenses came to $50,000. The above Asset Z's share of these expenses would be $6,250 ($50,000 x 0.125). This one allocation alone helps to reduce the tax on any gain derived by selling Asset Z.

Allocation of Intangibles

The same allocation principles in Figure 7.2 for tangibles also apply to the allocation of intangibles. The difference is that market values are more difficult to establish, if indeed they can be established at all. This leaves it up to the seller to compute the relative value of his intangibles the best way he can. We made some suggestions in this regard in Chapter 3: Determining Goodwill. We call this effort "seller valuing" rather than market valuing.

For example, consider a customer list. The seller has 600 customers with whom he has done business the past year. A good

85% are repeat customers over this past three to five years. In the most recent year alone, the customers provided $135,000 in gross sales to the business. Hence, the seller valued his customer list at $114,750 ($135,000 x 0.85).

Similarly, for a covenant not to compete. Suppose the seller were willing to grant a 5-year covenant which he estimated to be worth $5,000 per year. He determined this amount from the loss in sales from nonrepeat customers. He assumed that those customers who did not come back to him went to his competition. Obviously, in this case the seller's value of the covenant would be $25,000.

For his tax return purposes, the seller might value and categorize his intangibles as follows:

			Fraction
1.	Copyrights	$ 36,000	0.1305
2.	Distributorships	60,000	0.2175
3.	Customer lists	114,750	0.4161
4.	Noncompete covenant	25,000	0.0906
5.	Name & goodwill	40,000	0.1453
		$275,750	1.0000

The seller would make such a listing for himself for asking purposes. As long as he displayed a consistent rationale in computing these values, he could probably use them for relative fraction allocation purposes on his own tax return. Particularly so, if he acquired some of the intangibles separately and he carried them on his books as such. Most intangibles, however, are created by the owner of the business being sold. This can create allocation problems for the buyer after the sale. The buyer/acquirer of the assets has to set up his own books for capitalization, amortization, depreciation, and cost-of-goods accounting.

The "Whipsaw" Problem

For years, the IRS has complained that it was being whipsawed by the buyer and seller who were treating the allocation of assets differently, for the same transaction. Because certain assets, such as land and goodwill, for example, had to be capitalized on the buyer's books, this meant that the buyer's money was tied up and nonrecoverable. Naturally, the buyer wanted the allocation values of these items to be as low as possible. At the same time, he wanted the allocation values of those assets which could be depreciated, amortized, or expensed to be as high as possible. This meant that he could recover a larger portion of his purchase price than the IRS deemed proper.

In contrast, the seller wanted his allocation values to be just the opposite to those of the buyer. He wanted all capital assets to be allocably valued as high as possible. This meant that he could get capital gain treatment which is more tax advantageous than ordinary gain treatment. As to other assets, such as machinery, equipment, and inventory, the seller wanted their allocation values to be as low as possible. Because of depreciation recapture and other recapture rules, his preferred allocations could reduce his ordinary gain. This meant lower tax which also meant that the IRS was unhappy.

A depiction of the cross-purposes of allocation interests between buyer and seller — and the IRS — is presented in Figure 7.3 By "juggling" the allocation values, both buyer and seller could minimize their taxes independently of the other. After the sale, the IRS would come along and "reverse whipsaw" the allocation values so as to maximize the tax on both parties.

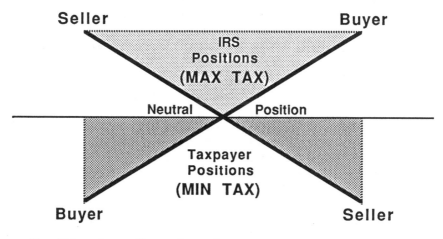

Fig. 7.3 - Cross-Purposing of Sale Price Allocation Interests

It wasn't long before business taxpayers caught on to the IRS's reverse whipsawing strategy. Spontaneously, they overwhelmed the IRS with a frenzy of buyouts, mergers, and acquisitions in the 1975-1985 period. Always ready for game, the IRS challenged every bulk transfer whose gross proceeds exceeded $100,000. As a result, the IRS became quagmired in problems of its own making. It appealed to Congress . . . whereupon a new tax law was born. That was in 1986.

Consistent Positions Required

The 1986 allocation law that came into being was Section 1060. It is titled: *Special Allocation Rules for Certain Asset Acquisitions.* The underlying thesis here is that **consistent positions** be taken by both buyer and seller. No longer could either party after the transaction revise its agreed allocations to suit its own tax purposes. The "certain asset acquisitions" are those where goodwill and going concern value attach to otherwise purely tangible assets. It was the goodwill factor that the IRS targeted unilaterally as being misstated.

In explaining its 1990 amendment to Section 1060, Congress — in its Conference Committee Report on P.L. 101-508 — wrote—

> *The bill provides that a written agreement regarding the allocation of consideration to, or the fair market value of, any of the assets in an applicable asset acquisition will be binding on both parties for tax purposes, unless the parties are able to refute the allocation or valuation standards set forth in the Danielson case. The parties are bound only with respect to the allocations or valuations actually provided in the agreement.*

> *It is not intended to restrict in any way the ability of the IRS to challenge the taxpayers' allocation to any asset or to challenge the taxpayers' determination of the fair market value of any asset by any appropriate method, particularly where there is a lack of adverse tax interests between the parties.*

The *Danielson* case referred to above is citable as: *C.L. Danielson*, CA-3, 67-1-USTC ¶ 9423, 378 F2d 771, Cert. denied, 389 U.S. 858. The focus of this landmark case was the agreed valuation of a covenant not to compete, which the IRS vigorously challenged. The IRS, it seems, always challenges covenants not to compete . . . just to be onerous. The Appeals Court (CA-3) held that—

> *Where the parties to a transaction involving the sale of a business have entered into an agreement spelling out the precise*

amount to be paid for a covenant not to compete, a party can challenge the tax consequences of this agreement as construed by the Commissioner [IRS] *only by adducing proof . . . to show its unenforceability because of **mistake, undue influence, fraud, duress**, and like reasons.* [Emphasis added.]

On remand, the Tax Court held that *Danielson*, the seller, was not fraudulently induced by the buyer to sign the noncompete agreement, and therefore the parties were bound by the agreement.

At the time of the *Danielson* case, there were 135 similar but unresolved cases that the IRS had challenged. Having lost on the issue, the IRS was not the least bit chagrined that it had tormented so many taxpayers for so long.

By referencing the *Danielson* case, Congress intended that the IRS not take a position inconsistent with a written agreement between the parties . . . unless there is a showing of mistake, undue influence, fraud, or duress.

Key Statutory Wording

Section 1060 of the Internal Revenue Code consists of just under 1,000 words. The key statutory wording therein is its subsection (a): General Rule. This general rule reads in full as—

In the case of any applicable asset acquisition, for purposes of determining both—

(1)   the transferee's basis in such assets, and
(2)   the gain or loss of the transferor with respect to such acquisition,

*the consideration received for such assets **shall be allocated** among such assets acquired in such acquisition in the same manner as amounts are allocated to assets under section 338(b)(5). If in connection with an applicable asset acquisition, the transferee and transferor **agree in writing** as to the allocation of any consideration, or as to the fair market value of any of the assets, such agreement **shall be binding** on both the transferee and transferor unless the* [IRS] *determines that such allocation (or fair market value) is not appropriate.* [Emphasis added.]

Presumably, the IRS will respect the intent of Congress and not undo arbitrarily the written agreement between buyer and seller. Presumably, also, the IRS will adopt the standards set by the *Danielson* case before attempting to redetermine the mutually agreed-upon valuations by the parties.

One of the recurring phrases in the general rule above is: "applicable asset acquisition." This is defined in subsection 1060(c) as—

Any transfer (whether directly or indirectly)—

(1)   of assets which constitute a trade or business, and
(2)   with respect to which the transferee's basis in such assets is determined wholly by reference to the consideration paid for such assets.

The point being made here is that Section 1060 is applicable only to businesses sold more or less in bulk, for their ongoing value. This, then, appears to put the primary burden on the transferee/acquirer to take the lead in insisting on a written allocation agreement. Preferably, this should be done at the time of the Contract of Sale. If there are potential valid reasons for changing the allocation values later, appropriate contingency clauses can be used.

Five Allocation Classes

Regulation 1.1060-1T(d) prescribes five specific allocation classes, namely: I, II, III, IV, and V. This regulation is titled: *Allocation of consideration among assets under the residual method*. Here, the term "residual method" refers to the subtractional sequences from the total consideration. From this total (which is the closing price), Class I assets are subtracted first, then Class II, then Class III, and then Class IV. Whatever remains after these subtractions — the residual — is Class V.

In more descriptive terms, the four allocation classes are:

Class I   — Cash, bank accounts, and equivalents.
Class II   — Marketable securities, foreign currency, certificates of deposit, U.S. bonds, etc.
Class III   — All other tangible and intangible assets except Classes IV and V.

Class IV   — All Section 197 intangibles except Class V.
Class V   — Goodwill and going concern value.

These allocation classes are those embodied in the above reference to "section 338(b)(5)" in Section 1060(a). The Class I and II designations are primarily applicable to large corporate takeovers where the swapping of publicly traded stock is much in vogue. This is self evident from the title of Section 338: *Certain Stock Purchases Treated as Asset Acquisitions*. Hence, Classes I and II are not likely to be significantly applicable to small business bulk sales. Classes III, IV, and V are definitely applicable.

Class III assets consist primarily of tangible items such as land, buildings, structures, furniture and fixtures, equipment, accounts receivable, and the like. Class IV assets consist primarily of covenant not to compete and other "separable intangibles": those non-197 intangibles listed in Figure 4.4 (on page 4-16). Whatever is left is Class V.

Obviously, for small business transfers, Classes III and IV are where all of the allocation action lies. As such, the seller and buyer are not without some flexibility as to their agreeing on the allocations. There is some range of fair market values for tangible assets that will satisfy the IRS. As for the *separable intangibles* (those separable from Class V), specific allocation values can be assigned when supported by cost acquisition data, contractual commitments, and computational estimates based on reasoned analysis. The objective in Classes III and IV is for the buyer and seller to do their own respective homework, and propose to each other the best mutually acceptable values. Unless there were a showing of collusion, fraud, duress, etc., such homework could make it more difficult for the IRS to arbitrarily redetermine the allocations.

Must Furnish to IRS

Prior to the enactment of Section 1060, the IRS's only bulk sale notification was Form 1099-S, discussed earlier. When it received a 1099-S showing an amount of gross proceeds over $100,000, it automatically contacted the seller to examine (audit) his return. At the outset of the examination, the IRS requested (demanded) the name and business address of the buyer. The examining agent then immediately contacted the buyer and examined his return also. The ostensible purpose was to examine both returns simultaneously to assure that the allocation values used were consistent. This required a lot of the IRS's time and effort, and stretched its resources.

Having its own lobbying staff in Washington, the IRS prevailed upon Congress to include a "must furnish" provision in Section 1060. For this, there was added subsection (b) titled: *Information Required to be Furnished to IRS.* This mandate reads as:

> *Under regulations, the transferor and transferee in an applicable asset acquisition shall, at such times and in such manner as may be provided in such regulations, furnish to the* [IRS] *the following information:*
>
> *(1) The amount of consideration received for the assets which is allocated to section 179 intangibles.*
> *(2) Any modification of the amount described in paragraph (1).*
> *(3) Any other information with respect to other assets transferred in such acquisition as the* [IRS] *deems necessary to carry out the provisions of this section.*

The IRS-prepared regulations on Section 1060 comprise approximately 6,500 words. In one particular subregulation — Reg. 1.1060-1T(e)(4) — the IRS carved out for itself special authority to undo what Congress intended and what the courts ruled on. This particular regulation reads in full as:

> *In connection with the examination of a return, the* [IRS] *may challenge the taxpayer's determination of the fair market value of any asset by any appropriate method and take into account all factors, including any lack of adverse tax interests between the parties. For example, in certain cases the IRS may make an independent showing of the value of goodwill and going concern value* **as a means of calling into question** *the validity of the taxpayer's valuation of other assets.* [Emphasis added.]

Thus, we're really back to "Square 1." The parties to a bulk sale have to furnish to the IRS all the pertinent information regarding their agreed allocations. After being so informed, the IRS has reserved the power unto itself to redetermine the allocations based on its own showing that some other value MAY apply. The IRS is well known in the business community for its revenue foraging through pure speculation.

Form 8594 Required

To its credit, the IRS has come up with a rather simple form for furnishing the information required by Section 1060(b). This is **Form 8594:** *Asset Acquisition Statement.* It is arranged in three parts, namely:

Part I   —   General Information
Part II   —   Assets Transferred (Classes I, II, III, IV, & V)
Part III —   Supplemental Statement (for an increase or decrease in consideration)

Our edited version of Form 8594 is presented in Figure 7.4. Note that we have intentionally omitted about 3" of full-width white space below Part II, and about 7" of white space below Part III. We signify all of these blank spaces as: *Footnotes and attachments.*

The official instructions to Form 8594 direct that it be prepared by *both* the buyer and the seller, and that a separate (duplicate) copy be attached to their separate income tax returns. The type of returns mentioned are: Forms 1040 (proprietorships), 1065 (partnerships), 1120 (corporations), and others similar. In Chapter 9: Sale of Proprietorship, we'll trail you through the attachment process. Similar procedures apply to partnerships and corporations.

As indicated in Figure 7.4, there are two checkboxes in the head portion of the form, namely: ☐ Buyer and ☐ Seller. The buyer is indicated first because of the title of the form: asset *acquisition*. Each party, however, must furnish the name, business address, and tax identification number of the other party. Also, the date of sale and total sale price must be stated.

We particularly call your attention in Figure 7.4 to the dollar-value columns of Part II. The two columns are:

(a)   Aggregate Fair Market Value, and
(b)   Allocation of Sales Price.

For each column, there is a separate line for each of the previously described classes of assets: I, II, III, IV, and V. The columnar

Form 8594	ASSET ACQUISITION STATEMENT	Year of Sale

Name, Tax ID, Tax Form No. □ 1040 □ 1065 □ 1120 □ other	□ Buyer □ Seller

Part I   General Information

Other Party's Name, Address, Tax ID _____

Date of Sale _____   Total Sales Price _____

Part II   Assets Transferred

Class	Fair Market Value	Allocation of Sales Price
I		
II		
III		
IV		
V		
Total		

Checkbox questions: □   □   □

Part III   Supplemental Statement

Asset Class	Previous Allocation	Increase <Decrease>	Redetermined Allocation
Total			

Footnotes and attachments

Fig. 7.4 - Edited Version of Asset Allocation Form 8594

principles involved are identical to the hypothetical example we presented back in Figure 7.2.

In addition to your filling in the four aggregate class lines in Part II, we suggest that you attach an itemized listing of your Class IV intangibles. This is the one category guaranteed to be examined by the IRS. This is because most sellers tend to be cavalier about their separately acquired and/or self-created assets. They don't think through and spend the time to develop the supporting rationale for their cost assignments and allocations.

Checkbox Questions Asked

The lower portion of Part II of Form 8594 has three checkbox questions which you must answer ☐ Yes or ☐ No. Leaving them blank is the same as answering them "No." A "No" answer means that you have not complied with the general rule of Section 1060(a) quoted earlier.

In Figure 7.4, for space reasons, we omitted the actual checkbox questions. We'll quote them for you now:

- *Did the buyer and seller provide for an allocation of the sales price in the sales contract or in another written document signed by both parties?* ☐ *Yes* ☐ *No*

- *If "Yes" are the aggregate fair market values listed for each of asset Classes I, II, III, IV, and V the amounts agreed upon in your sales contract or in a separate written document?* ☐ *Yes* ☐ *No*

- *Did the buyer also purchase a license or a covenant not to compete, or enter into a lease agreement, employment contract, management contract, or similar arrangement with the seller?* ☐ *Yes* ☐ *No*

- *If "Yes," specify (a) the type of agreement, and (b) the maximum amount of consideration (not including interest) paid or to be paid under the agreement.*

From the tone of these questions, can't you imagine what will happen if you answer "No" or leave them blank? Your tax return *will be* examined (audited). Count on it! This is the whole purpose of these three questions. Whether you answer them "Yes" or "No", be prepared for audit. A "Yes" does not guarantee against an audit; it simply challenges the IRS to test you . . . at its risk.

Class IV Intangibles: Itemize

A particular target intended on Form 8594 is your Class IV intangibles. Especially those which are not separately acquired before the sale and which are not amortizable under specific sections of the tax code other than Section 197. Because of the difficulty of establishing the fair market values of these intangibles, the IRS would like you to itemize them in an attachment to Part II of the form. This way, it can pick and choose which values it wants to attack. It *will* attack those which are amortized less than 15 years.

Be sure to obtain the latest official version of **Form 8594** and its instructions. Read carefully the definition of Class IV and Class V assets. These two classes are grouped together as "Section 197 intangibles." The grouping includes:

- *Goodwill*
- *Going concern value*
- *Workforce in place*
- *Business books and records, operating systems, or other information base*
- *Any patent, copyright, formula, process, design, pattern, know-how, format, or similar item*
- *Any customer-based intangible*
- *Any supplier-based intangible*
- *Any license, permit, or other right granted by a governmental unit*
- *Any covenant not to compete entered into in connection with the acquisition of an interest in a trade or business, and*
- *Any franchise (other than a sports franchise), trademark, or trade name.*

With such all inclusiveness (subject to 15-year amortization), you are well advised to use "diligent effort" when valuing any Section 197 intangible.

To exemplify what we mean by diligent effort, suppose you had obtained a copyright to a technical book or computer manual that you had created. To register the copyright, it cost you $20. Would you sell it for that amount? What about your labor and time?

To establish a market value for your copyright, you have to reconstruct how many actual hours were spent on the project. How many hours did you put in it; how many hours do you pay others to do portions of it. Let's say that you can show that a total of 500 hours was spent on creating the copyrighted item. Next, you show the range of hourly billing rates that you paid or would have had to pay to others to do similar work. Suppose the average rate is $50 per hour. With this information, you would be able to show that the value of your copyright is $25,000 (500 hrs x $50/hr).

For every intangible asset that you identify in Class IV, you want to have strong calculational background. You should be prepared to support your valuations . . . should the IRS come calling. A "teaser" in this respect is to attach to Form 8594 an itemization of these assets with the computed value of each item displayed. Then place a little headnote or footnote: *Computations available for each item listed.*

After-Sale Reallocations

The principal allocation-of-sales-price action takes place in Part II of Form 8594: *Assets Transferred.* Said allocations (between classes and between items within each class) are predicated upon the agreed total sales price at the time the sale actually closes. Form 8594, however, is prepared after the sale, and after the taxable year ends in which the sale took place. After financial, tax, and legal reality sets in, it is not uncommon for "adustments" to the total sales price to be made. This is where Part III of Form 8594: *Supplemental Statement*, takes on a role of its own.

The purpose of Part III is to allow the seller and buyer to each settle down and take a hard look at what they have done. Each has different post-sale tax and financial interests. Each does his own postings and trial runs on his books of account. Often, this entails one or more adjustments (increases or decreases) to (a) total sales price, (b) class allocations, and/or (c) allocations within each class. The instructions to Form 8594 require that, in such event, **reallocations** be made. On this point, the instructions say—

> *If the increase or decrease occurs in the same tax year as the purchase date, consider the increase or decrease to have occurred on the purchase date. If the increase or decrease occurs after the tax year of the purchase date, consider it in the tax year in which it occurs.*

The instructions for reallocating increases require that they apply to Class V assets last. Conversely, when reallocating decreases, apply them to Class V assets first. The IRS is particularly sensitive about seller and buyer manipulaitng Class IV and Class V items for the best tax advantage to both sides. The possibilities for manipulation can be surmised from our depiction in Figure 7.5.

For the seller, Form 8594 becomes the reference base for determining his gain or loss on each asset (or category of assets)

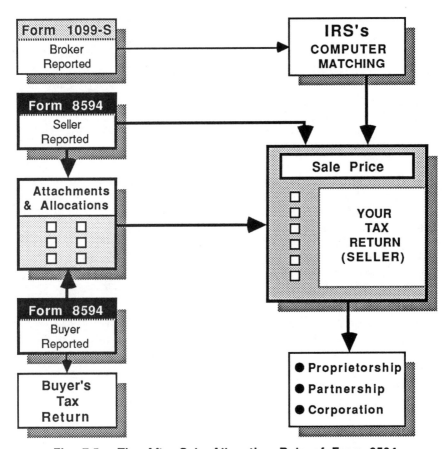

Fig. 7.5 - The After-Sale Allocation Role of Form 8594

sold. Even though transferred in bulk, there are no gain or loss bulk tax schedules that attach to a return. Therefore, each separate asset category has to be tax-traced-through on its own.

As for the buyer, he needs Form 8594 and its attachments to set up his capital accounts, depreciation accounts, amortization accounts, inventory accounts, expense accounts, and other matters. But since this is a book on *selling* a business, not on buying one, we will not go any further into the buyer's tax interests in the sale. Accordingly, the chapters which follow will deal strictly with the seller's tax return obligations.

8

THE MASTER FORM: 4797

> From Form 8594 (In Chapter 7), Transfers Are Made Asset-By-Asset Onto Form 4797. This Form Is Necessary For Determining, Separately, The Gain Or Loss On EACH ASSET (or Class Of Assets), And For Converting The Net Gain To Capital Gain, And The Net Loss To Ordinary Income. This SPECIAL TREATMENT Is Afforded Only To Business-Use Property By Section 1231. Because "Recapture Rules" Apply, Certain Items Have To Be Entered Into Part III, Before Completing Parts I And II Of Form 4797. The Results Of Part I (Capital Gain) And Of Part II (Ordinary Income) Are Entered As INCOME On Your Year-Of-Sale Tax Return.

Form 4797 is titled: *Sales of Business Property*. It attaches directly to the income tax returns of proprietorships, partnerships, and corporations (also estates and trusts). It is one of the most — if not THE most — versatile tax form in the IRS's catalog of about 600 forms. It is the "hub form" for reconciliation of all asset schedules prepared prior to the sale, and for distributing gain or loss information to other schedules after the sale. This is why we call it the *master* form when selling a business.

Active businesses sell products and services on a daily basis. These are called sales in the *ordinary* course of a trade or business. Such sales do not appear on Form 4797. They appear on other regular schedules of a tax return. Form 4797 is to be used only for sales of property (tangible and intangible) which do not constitute the "ordinary" course of business. After all, if the assets of a business are sold in bulk or nearly so, there is no business left to conduct on a daily basis.

So, in this chapter we want to share with you the marvels of Form 4797. It is of key and utmost importance to the preparation of your income tax return after your business is sold. There is no other alternate form that you can use. For this reason, we want you to be aware of it, and be knowledgeable about it. Since an owner does not sell a business (in bulk) every day — or every year — Form 4797 does not have the general usage of other more common tax forms and schedules. Consequently, even if you already know of the form, we suspect that you could use a little refresher on the mechanics of it.

General Purpose: Gross Proceeds

The official instructions to Form 4797 state that its purpose is—

To report:

• *The sale or exchange of trade or business property; depreciable and amortizable property; oil, gas, geothermal, or other mineral properties; and section 126* [farm] *property.*

• *The disposition of other noncapital assets.*

This purpose obviously has been condensed to its official heading on the form, namely: ***Sales of Business Property.***

Thus, the primary purpose of Form 4797 is to report the sale of a business and other related assets. The form is structured into Gain and Loss columns, with separate line entries for each asset or category of assets sold. This structuring alone attests to its purpose as being the determination of the tax-accountable gain or loss on those assets that were transferred to the buyer of your business. At the end of each gain and loss column, there are subtotaling lines with printed-thereon instructions directing you to other forms and schedules We'll get to these transferral instructions later.

We're telling you right off that there is an ambiguity when you read the long headnote instruction at the top of the form (just below the entry line for your name and Tax ID number). This particular instruction reads:

Enter here the gross proceeds from the sale or exchange of real estate reported to you on Form(s) 1099-S (or a substitute statement) that you will be including [hereon]. [Emphasis added.]

The ambiguity is that the heading on the form says "business property" whereas the headnote instruction says "real estate." We explained this apparent inconsistency back in Chapter 7. For reasons given earlier, the sale of a business is tax classed as a "real estate transaction." This is so that the gross proceeds of the sale reported to the IRS on Form 1099-S can be electronically transmitted long before the seller gets around to preparing his tax return and reporting the same sales figure amount.

Note in the instruction above that we emphasized the phrase: **or a substitute statement.** Would not a "substitute statement" include Form 8594: Asset Acquisition Statement? Of course it does. Form 8594 shows an entry for: *Total sale price.* You had better hope — or see to it — that these two reported figures for the same business sale are identical in their dollar amounts. Otherwise, the wrath of the IRS computer will be on your back!

Let us explain.

In the upper right-hand corner of Form 4797, immediately below your Tax ID number, there is one — just **one** — bulk entry box. It is directly across from the headnote instruction that starts

with: *Enter here* .... 1 $

This is the only place on your entire tax return that you can enter the total sale price (gross proceeds) of your business.

What do you suppose would happen if your Form 1099-S showed a gross proceeds figure of $365,000 and your Form 8594 showed a total sale price of $350,000? Such inconsistencies happen all the time when reporting tax information by different individuals, under different pressures.

Answer: The IRS's Big Computer would **add** the two figures together, and send you a proposed assessment of tax on $715,000 (365,000 + 350,000). This will get your attention!

By now you must surely realize that there is one *instant purpose* of Form 4797. It is to provide one-only entry box for showing the gross selling price of your business. This is the only place on your return that the IRS's computer can look to, to match the amount that you report with the amounts reported on Forms 1099-S and 8594. If you miss reporting the correct amount, you are off to a bad start in your sale-of-business tax accounting.

Format Overview: Parts I, II, & III

Form 4797 consists of two full pages, front and back, each with lines and columns. It is arranged into three parts, namely:

Part I   — Property Held More than 1 Year
Part II   — Ordinary Gains and Losses
Part III — Gain from Disposition of [Recapture] Property

Parts I and II are on page 1; Part III takes most all of page 2.

A general overview of the format of Form 4797 is presented in Figure 8.1. Obviously, the presentation is not a duplication of the official form. Therefore, it is suggested that you request a copy of the official form (and its instructions) from the IRS Forms Center serving your area. You should have it handy as a reference, even though you yourself may not fill it out.

Do note in Figure 8.1 that we have emphasized the one-only entry block for the total sale price (gross proceeds) of your bulk transaction. The official form does not emphasize this "computer homing device" the way we have done. Because it is so innocuous looking on the official form, many taxpayers miss it altogether. Note particularly that this one block stands alone. There are no gain or loss columns associated with it as there are in Parts I and II.

Part I consists of horizontal lines broken into eight columnar segments. One asset, or one category of assets, is entered on each line along with other data for determining the net gain or loss for that asset. These, with their eight columns, are called the direct entry lines. There are also indirect entry lines which have only two columns: gain or loss. They are "indirect" in that the entries are transferred from other forms, or from other parts of Form 4797 itself.

The format of Part II is essentially similar to that of Part I. There are a few more indirect entry lines which we'll explain later. The main difference between Parts I and II is that only those capital or depreciable type assets *held more than 1 year* go into Part I; all others go into Part II.

Part III is the most difficult portion of the form to understand. Its official title is: ***Gain from Disposition of Property under***

Form 4797	SALES OF BUSINESS PROPERTY						Year	
Name _____							Tax ID No.	

Enter GROSS PROCEEDS ▶ ▶ ▶ ▶ ▶ ▶ [1 | $]

PART I - Property Held More Than 1 Year

(a)	(b)	(c)	(d)	(e)	(f)	(g)	(h)
	Direct Entries						
	Indirect Entries						

PART II - Ordinary Gains and Losses

(a)	(b)	(c)	(d)	(e)	(f)	(g)	(h)
	Direct Entries						
	Indirect Entries						

PART III - Gain From Recapture Property

	A	B	C	D
Recapture Instructions				

Summary Part III: Enter recapture in Part II
                   Enter excess gain in Part I

(Other matters on official form)

Fig. 8.1 - Functional Overview of Form 4797: Parts I and II

Sections 1245, 1250, 1252, 1254, and 1255. Earlier, we simply listed this as "recapture" property. Special recapture rules apply which are prescribed in the tax code sections enumerated. We'll give you the essence of these recapture rules later.

The 8 Columns Identified

In Figure 8.1 we purposely omitted the eight columnar headings (in Parts I and II) that appear on the official form We simply indicated them as columns (a), (b), (c), etc. We want to identify them for you now.

The eight columnar headings are:

(a)   Description of property

(b) Date acquired (month, day, year)
(c) Date sold (month, day, year)
(d) Gross sale price (**as allocated**)
(e) Depreciation allowed or allowable since acquisition
(f) Cost or other basis, plus improvements and expense of sale (as allocated)
(g) LOSS: col. (f) minus the sum of cols. (d) and (e)
(h) GAIN: cols. (d) plus (e) minus col. (f)

All except columns (e) and (f), we believe, are self-explanatory. However, all require that you do some homework and reconstruct entry information from prior tax schedules and worksheets, and from Form 8594.

Column (e): Depreciation "allowed or allowable" since acquisition pertains to the use of *straight line* depreciation only. If you used other than straight line — that is, any form of accelerated depreciation — you must use Part III. You cannot show that asset in Part I. The term "depreciation" also includes amortization which, by definition, is purely straight line. The effect of column (e) is to *recapture* all straight-line depreciation and amortization as capital gain at time of sale. The greater the amount of this recapture, the greater the gain from the disposition.

Column (f): Cost or other basis, plus improvement and expense of sale is the "workhorse" column on Form 4797. It can either minimize your gain or maximize your loss. Either way, it means going back to your records when you first acquired the asset being sold. If you purchased the item, your initial basis is its cost. If you did not purchase the item, but acquired it through an exchange, gift, or inheritance, you must use the basis rules for such acquisitions. Thereafter, you add all capital-type improvements (not repairs or maintenance) that will enhance your basis. To this combined amount, you add the allocable portion of your gross selling expenses.

Recall from Figure 8.1 that the eight entry columns appear in Parts I and II only. The Part I entries are for those assets held for more than one year; the Part II entries are for those held one year or less. This is where columns (b): date acquired, and (c) date sold, become important. To figure the one-year period, begin counting on the day *after* you acquired the item and *include* the day you sold it. Because of the tax benefits when holding more than one year, if you are near the one-year mark, intentionally delay the sale.

Section 1231:   Very Special

Before we tell you more about Parts I and II, we want to tell you about Section 1231. The section is titled (in part): *Property Used in the Trade or Business*. For properties held more than one year, Section 1231 is known as the "capital gain, ordinary loss" rule. The end effect is that if, in Part I, the losses exceed the gains, the net losses go to Part II to become ordinary losses rather than capital losses.

For qualified transactions (explained below), the *capital gain, ordinary loss* rule is the best of both tax worlds. When the gains exceed losses in Part I, the net gain is treated as capital gain This is advantageous because the gain can be used to offset other capital losses elsewhere on a return, after which the net capital gain is taxed at a lower rate than ordinary gain. When the losses exceed gains in Part I, the net loss goes to Part II where it is treated as an ordinary loss. This, too, is advantageous, as ordinary losses are not limited in amount as are capital losses. The only limit to ordinary losses is the extent of one's other positive income sources on a return.

Subsection 1231(a)(3)(B) defines a "Section 1231 loss" as—

Any recognized loss from a sale or exchange . . . of property used in a trade or business.

Subsection 1231(a)(4)(A) then goes on to say—

The section 1231 losses shall be included only if and to the extent taken into account in computing taxable income, except that section 1211 shall not apply.

The reference to Section 1211 is: *Limitation on Capital Losses*. For individuals (proprietorships, partnerships, and S corporations), the limitation is $3,000 per year. For C corporations, the limitation is the extent of whatever capital gains there are. By decreeing for Section 1231 purposes that Section 1211 does not apply, the tax code has recharacterized capital losses from the sale of a business into ordinary losses. The only limitation to ordinary losses is . . . "to the extent taken into account in computing taxable income." In other words, if the losses are large enough, one's taxable income could be reduced to zero.

Qualified Section 1231 Property

To take advantage of the capital gain, ordinary loss rule of Section 1231, the property must be that which is used in a trade or business. Subsection 1231(b)(1) defines such property as being—

Of a character which is subject to an allowance for depreciation . . . held for more than 1 year, and real property used in the trade or business, held for more than 1 year, which is not—

(A) of a kind properly includible in inventory . . . at the close of the taxable year,
(B) held . . . primarily for sale to customers in the ordinary course of . . . business, or
(C) a copyright, a literary, musical or artistic composition, a letter or memorandum, or similar property, held by a taxpayer . . . whose personal efforts created such property.
[Emphasis added.]

(The "of a character" of depreciation also includes amortization.)

Thus, **except** for inventory, merchandise, and copyrights, all of those business-type assets — tangibles and intangibles — that we covered in previous chapters qualify as Section 1231 property. This includes goodwill, covenants not to compete, patents, licenses, franchises, leaseholds, etc. Why copyrights are excluded, whereas patents are not, has always been a mystery.

Also included as Section 1231 property are timber, coal, and iron ore; cattle, horses, and livestock (when held for draft, breeding, dairy, or sporting purposes); and unharvested crop (when sold with its land). [Sec. 1231(b)(2), (3), & (4).]

There is just one "tax catch" in the rosy scenario of Section 1231. The catch is that certain net Section 1231 losses are subject to **recapture**. The principle of "recapture" is the taking back of certain tax benefits previously enjoyed. The recapture rules are prescribed in subsection 1231(c): *Recapture of Net Ordinary Losses*. Its essence is—

The net section 1231 gain for any taxable year shall be treated as ordinary income to the extent such gain does not exceed the nonrecaptured net section 1231 losses . . . for the five most recent preceding taxable years.

In other words, if, within a period of five years before the current sale of your business, you sold other Section 1231 property and had net losses therefrom, the prior losses claimed as ordinary losses are subject to recapture. The "recapture" is by converting some of the net capital gain from your current sale to ordinary gain. The mechanics for doing so are directed by preprinted instructional lines on the lower portion of Part I of Form 4797. Prior to executing these conversion instructions, however, you are expected to complete Part III, if it is applicable.

Part III: Must Recapture

Part III is used to compute the recapture of depreciation and certain other items that must be reported as ordinary income upon the disposition of designated property. The "designated property" is that which is expressly prescribed in Sections 1245, 1250, 1252, 1254, and 1255 of the IR Code. The official headings to these sections are:

Sec. 1245 — *Gain from disposition of certain depreciable property*
Sec. 1250 — *Gain from disposition of certain depreciable realty*
Sec. 1252 — *Gain from disposition of farm land*
Sec. 1254 — *Gain from disposition of interest in oil, gas, geothermal, or other mineral properties*
Sec. 1255 — *Gain from disposition of* [certain cost-sharing] *property*

Note that all section titles lead off with the phrase: "Gain from disposition of." This is why Part III itself is officially titled: ***Gain from Disposition of Property under Sections 1245, 1250, 1252, 1254, and 1255***. If there is a loss on the disposition, said property item does **not** appear in Part III. It appears in Parts I or II. Otherwise, Part III is for computing the amount of recapture on *gain* dispositions only, and only if the property has been held more than one year. The rationale for recapture is that, while the designated properties were being held, they were allowed special expense writeoffs. When the property is sold at a gain, there is ordinary income "payback" to be made.

For overview purposes, we present in Figure 8.2 a highly simplified version of Part III. You'll know that it is "simplified"

Form 4797	GAIN FROM DISPOSITION OF RECAPTURE PROPERTY	Part III
Under Sections 1245, 1250, 1252, 1254, 1255		

Description of Property	"A"	"B"
● Each separate property asset		
● Held more than 1 year	"C"	"D"
● Date acquired; date sold		

Computation of Gain	
1. Gross sale price	
2. Cost or other basis plus expense of sale	
3. Depreciation or depletion allowed or allowable	
4. Adjusted basis: subtract 3 from 2	
5. Total gain: subtract 4 from 1	

● **Section 1245** - Depreciation of machinery & equipment	
● **Section 1250** - Additional depreciation of buildings	
● **Section 1252** - Conservation expenses: farmland	
● **Section 1254** - Intangible drilling & development costs	
● **Section 1255** - Subsidy payments excluded from income	

Summary of part III Gains	
6. Total gain all properties	_____
7. Total of recapture income ● Enter here & on Part II (ordinary)	_____
8. Subtract 7 from 6 ● Enter here & on Part I (capital)	_____

Fig. 8.2 - General Arrangement of Form 4797: Part III

once you compare Figure 8.2 with an official form. For the moment, we just want to familiarize you with its general arrangement. As you can see, it accommodates four separate properties. If the bulk disposition of your business constitutes more than four applicable assets, use additional Part III's. The total gain on each asset is computed separately in a simplified 5-step sequence. We show these five steps in the upper half of Figure 8.2.

The midsection of Figure 8.2 lists the five property classes for which recapture is required. For computing the recapture portion of each property gain, there are preprinted instructional lines on the official form. The five classes are:

Sec. 1245 — Depreciable tangible property (such as furniture, appliances, machinery, equipment, etc.) for which *any* kind of depreciation was taken.

Sec. 1250 — Depreciable real property (such as buildings, structures, and their improvements) for which *additional* depreciation (meaning "accelerated" beyond straight-line) was taken.

Sec. 1252 — Farmland held for less than 10 years for which conservation expenditures (such as soil, water, and reforestation efforts) were expensed rather than capitalized.

Sec. 1254 — Resource land on which intangible drilling and development costs were expensed rather than amortized over 10 years or more.

Sec. 1255 — Farmland held for less than 20 years for which government subsidy payments were previously excluded from gross income.

At the bottom of Figure 8.2, there are three steps showing how the total gain from all properties (aggregated together) is split between recapture income (ordinary gain) and capital gain. As indicated, the capital gain goes onto Part I and the recapture income goes onto Part II. This explains why, if applicable, you have to complete Part III before completing Parts I and II.

Parts I and II Revisited

Going back now to Parts I and II, we present in Figure 8.3 a more expanded version of these parts than was presented in Figure 8.1. This time we are showing the specific lines (highly edited) for the indirect entries. The "indirect" entries are so-called because they originate from other forms and from other parts of Form 4797 itself.

The most significant of these other forms are:

Form 4684: Casualties and Thefts
Form 6252: Installment Sale Income
Form 8824: Like-Kind Exchanges

Form 4797	SALES OF BUSINESS PROPERTY					Year	
Attach To Form 1040, 1065, 1120, as appropriate							
PART I - Property Held More Than 1 Year							
(a)	(b)	(c)	(d)	(e)	(f)	(g)	(h)
						LOSS	GAIN
			DIRECT ENTRIES				
● Gain from Form 4684						▨	
● Gain from Form 6252						▨	
● Gain/Loss from Form 8824						▨	
● Capital Gain, Part III						▨	
● Sec.1231 losses: prior years							▨
ADD COLUMNS (g) AND (h): NET ⟶							▢
IF GAIN, enter on Schedule D IF LOSS, enter on Part II							
PART II - Ordinary Gains and Losses							
			DIRECT ENTRIES				
● Loss from Part I							▨
● Recapture Sec. 1231 gain						▨	
● Recapture Income, Part III						▨	
● Gain/Loss from Form 4684							
● Ordinary Gain, Form 6252						▨	
● Gain/Loss from Form 8824							
● Sec. 179 recapture						▨	
ADD COLUMNS (g) AND (h): NET ⟶							▢
Enter on Page 1 of Form 1040, 1065, 1120, as appropriate							

Fig. 8.3 - General Arrangement of Form 4797: Parts I and II

We are not going to discuss these forms; we list them to indicate the great versatility of Form 4797. Also indicated for Part II is a separate line entry for: "Section 179 recapture." Section 179 is a special first-year election to expense certain productive tangible assets used in business. When the business use of these assets falls to 50% or below, the previously expensed amounts are recaptured.

The Figure 8.3 arrangement (Parts I and II) consists primarily of two columns: LOSS and GAIN. The entries in each column are added and subtotaled for that column in Part I and, separately, in Part II. Then the loss and gain subtotals are combined to produce a net loss or net gain. There is a net loss **or** net gain for Part I and, separately, a net loss **or** net gain for Part II. In the figure, we have emphasized the one net box in each part.

As a reminder, Part I is intended primarily for the disposition of Section 1231 property. This applies, even though some of the gain from certain property items is subject to recapture in Part III. If an item or asset does not qualify as Section 1231 property, it can be entered in Part II. For example, whereas the sale or transfer of a patent would be entered in Part I, the sale or transfer of a copyright would be entered in Part II. Similarly for inventory, merchandise, unexpired leases, employee contracts, and other "odds and ends" when selling off a business.

As a matter of practice, Part II of Form 4797 is a *catchall.* It can be used for entering all kinds of dispositional items, whenever there is no other clear-cut place on a tax return for entering them. For example, suppose, when preparing your business for sale, you abandoned some of your accounts receivable as being noncollectible. You can enter your abandonment loss in Part II. Similarly, for obsolete and damaged items, or miscellaneous tools and supplies that you may have been carrying on your books at scrap value. Very few business owners and sellers fully comprehend the all-purpose clearing-the-books virtues of Part II.

Transfers from Form 4797

Form 4797 is not a final tax computation schedule on its own. For such tax it serves an intermediate role. Its sole purpose is to establish the net gain or net loss — capital (Part I) **and** ordinary (Part II) — from a series of business-use assets sold or exchanged either in bulk or piecemeal. The net gain or net loss established is transferred to other forms and schedules where it combines with other sources of income before the final tax is computed. Where on other forms/schedules do the Form 4797 results go? It depends on the operating form of your business entity: proprietorship, partnership, or corporation.

In Figure 8.3, the long black arrow in Part I and, separately, in Part II points to a single *result box*. Alongside of and below each result box, there are preprinted instructions as to where the results are to be transferred. These instructions address partnerships first, S corporations next, and all others last. Here, the term "all others" includes individuals, proprietorships, estates, trusts, and C corporations.

Editorial Note: There is a distinction between an S corporation and a C corporation that is pertinent here. An S corporation is a pass-through entity (like a partnership) whereas a C corporation is not. The "pass-through" feature means that the transferred amounts wind up *directly* on the seller's individual **Form 1040**. While a C corporation's results also wind up on Form 1040, the pathway is via Schedule D alone: not Form 4797.

For partnerships and S corporations, the **Part I** transfer instructions read (in edited form):

Partnerships   — *Enter the gain or loss on Form 1065, Schedule K (follow the instructions).*

S Corporations — *Report the gain or loss on Form 1120S, Schedule K (follow the instructions).*

As to **All others**, the **Part I** instructions read (again, in edited form):

If the [result box] *is zero or a loss, enter the amount* [in Part II] *below. If the* [amount] *is a gain and you did not have any prior year section 1231 losses, or they were recaptured in an earlier year, enter the gain as a long-term capital gain on Schedule D* [Capital Gains and Losses].

The essence of this instruction is that if the result box is more than zero (with no nonrecaptured Section 1231 losses), the result amount is capital gain. If it is zero or a loss, the resultant amount is converted to ordinary loss (in Part II). This is the net effect of our diagrammatic presentation in Figure 8.4. Believe it or not, for sales

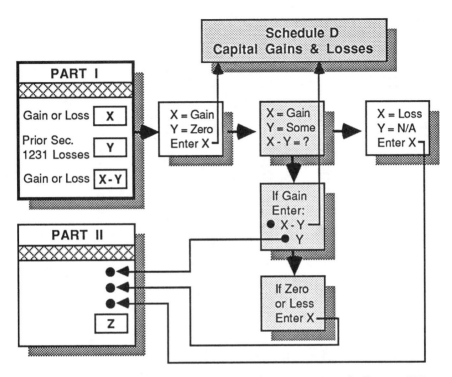

Fig. 8.4 - The Intended Flow of Results From Part I, Form 4797

of business property held more than one year, you are getting the best of both tax worlds.

The Part II transfer instructions alongside of its result box are straightforward. The instructions simply say: *Enter the* [result box] *gain or loss on the return being filed.*

On each return "being filed" — proprietorship, partnership, or corporation — the Part II amount goes to an entry line labeled:

- *Other gain or loss. Attach Form 4797* [proprietorships]
- *Net gain or loss from Form 4797* [partnerships, etc.]

Focal Role Summarized

Note in Figure 8.4 that the *gain* portion of Part I goes to a Schedule D: Capital Gains and Losses. There is a Schedule D

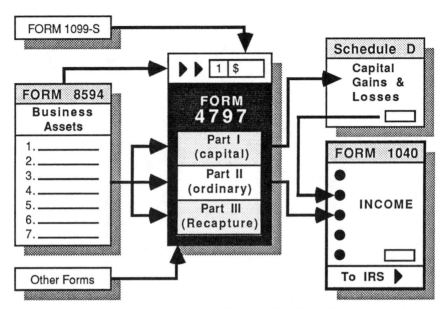

Fig. 8.5 - Focal Role of Form 4797 After-The-Sale

(1040) for proprietorships, a Schedule D (1065) for partnerships, and a Schedule D (1120) for corporations. Each of these schedules has a line labeled: *Enter gain from Form 4797.* This enables the Form 4797 capital gain to be added to, or to be offset by, other capital gains and losses of the pre-sale activities of the business being sold. This is further manifestation of the favorable tax benefits flowing from Form 4797.

In contrast, Part II, which is *ordinary* gain *or* loss, goes directly onto the page 1 income of Forms 1040, 1065, and 1120. There it combines with other positives and negatives, to be added to (or be offset by) them. Again, these are benefits flowing from Form 4797.

We cannot overstress the focal importance of Form 4797. In one sense, it is a receptacle for information from Forms 1099-S and 8594 (and other forms). In still another sense, it is a two-part distributor to other entries that make up one's business tax return. We depict this role with emphasis, in Figure 8.5. When selling your business, Form 4797 is truly THE FORM that you should master.

9

SALE OF PROPRIETORSHIP

A Proprietorship Sale Is Selling Either A Schedule C Business Or A Schedule F Business, Or Both. If Reported On A Joint (Husband And Wife) Form 1040, A Separate Spousal Tax ID Is Required For Each Business Sold, And On All Related Forms, Such As 8594 (Asset Statement), 4797 (Sale Of Business), 6252 (Installment Sale), 8824 (Like-Kind Exchange), And 4562 (Depreciation & Amortization). The History Of Each Asset Sold Goes On A COST RECOVERY WORKSHEET, With all Expenses Of The Sale Allocated. Preparation Of The 1040 Necessitates Three Entry Phases, Namely: I - Pre-Sale, II - THE SALE, And III - Post-Sale.

A proprietorship is the simplest form of doing business. It is so because it is a one owner business. The owner can decide whether, and when, to sell without consultation with any co-owner. It is for this reason that a proprietorship is also referred to as a *sole proprietorship*.

If the proprietor is married, there is a "co-owner" in a sense. This is so whether the spouse works in the business or not. Nevertheless, for tax purposes, the business is still treated as a sole proprietorship. There are two reasons for this. One, a husband and wife are treated as one taxpayer when filing a joint Form 1040.

The other reason is that the net earnings from the business are subject to self-employment tax (social security and medicare). A social security account is ascribed to one person only. If the spouse wants to build up a separate social security account of his or her own, there need to be *two* separate proprietorship businesses. Such an arrangement is workable when filing a joint Form 1040.

For proprietorship purposes, there are two business entity schedules which attach to Form 1040. These are:

Schedule C (1040) — Profit or Loss from Business
Schedule F (1040) — Profit or Loss from Farming

When either business, or both, are sold, there are associated pre-sale schedules that have to be updated and posted. And, of course, after the sale, there is Form 8594 (in Chapter 7) and Form 4797 (in Chapter 8) to be prepared . . . and brought forward.

In this chapter, we want to illustrate with specific numbers how the sale of a proprietorship business is addressed and reported on a joint Form 1040. For this purpose, we are going to assume that the husband operates a Schedule C activity, while the wife separately operates a Schedule F activity. We will also assume that both proprietorships are sold in the same year, but not necessarily at the same time. The reasons for selling are not tax relevant.

The Pre-Sale Scenario

A proprietorship is a basic form of business. As such, its sale exposes the owner to all the tax elements of a larger business, whether it be in partnership or corporate form. Thus, the sale of a proprietorship provides a good starting example of the tax ramifications that follow upon the sale of any business.

For our selected example, we have a husband and wife, each having his and her own separate proprietorship. He's an arson investigator filing a Schedule C; she's a horse breeder filing a Schedule F. They each keep their own business books separately, but they assist each other in business as needed. They file Form 1040 jointly. They own a home, but the home is not being sold. He rents office space in town; she rents a small ranch with boarding stables outside of town. Other than receiving some interest and dividends, they have no other significant sources of income.

The husband was formerly a fire captain, but has been a self-employed arson investigator for more than five years. His business has steadily increased in profits over the years. His Schedule C assets consist of an off-road truck which he drives to fire scenes wherever they may be. The truck can be used as a one-person camper for up to five days, while at fire scenes out of town. He has the typical office furniture and equipment (computer, printer, copier, fax, typewriter, answering machine, etc.). He also has some very special hand tools and electronic instruments for gathering samples and evidence. He maintains contact with various fire consultants and laboratories for the testing and analyzing of large samples and special items. He has developed his own procedural work manual and know-how (which he copyrighted). After his analysis of the cause and origin of a fire is made, he makes a written report of his findings and recommendations. His customers are local fire departments, insurance companies, and agents who write fire insurance contracts. The husband is professionally licensed but his license is not transferable.

As a horse breeder, the wife was born and reared on a ranch and began breeding premium horses after being married for several years. She has been running her own boarding and breeding business for the past seven years. Her Schedule F assets consist of a heavy-duty truck for hauling (separately) two horse trailers. Even though she rents pasture land and stables, she has her own training equipment, saddle gear, feeding facilities, and corrals. She has one registered stallion and three registered brood mares. When she breeds foals, she keeps them two to three years before selling them. She rents out her stallion and collects stud fees. She is a member of the American Quarter Horse Association (AQHA) and advertises regularly in its monthly publication. Because her Schedules F have shown losses several years in a row, she has been audited by the IRS repeatedly. However, there have been no changes to her tax returns as filed.

The husband sold his business in the first half of the year; the wife sold her business in the latter half of the same year. The husband's business (Schedule C) sold for $250,000; the wife's business (Schedule F) sold for $165,000. Each sale was a separate contract of its own.

The Schedule C Sale

For tax purposes, the primary interest in a sales contract is threefold, namely:

One.   The asset allocation of the total sale price — for itemizing on Form 8594, which buyer and seller must agree to;

Two. The terms of the sale if not all cash — for economic reality and market rates of interest;

Three. The personal services of the seller that continue after the sale on behalf of the buyer — for assessing any distortion of the allocations.

For the Schedule C example postulated above, the $250,000 sale price is allocated as follows:

	Amount	Fraction
1. Truck & accessories	$ 35,000	0.1400
2. Fire tools & instruments	25,000	0.1000
3. Office furniture & equipment	5,000	0.0200
4. Copyrighted fire manual	15,000	0.0600
5. Customer list (3 yrs)	30,000	0.1200
6. Consulting contract (1 yr)	60,000	0.2400
7. Goodwill, etc.	80,000	0.3200
	$250,000	1.0000

Although not always done, it is a good idea to show in the contract the fraction of each asset allocation relative to the total sale price. For one reason, it provides a quantitative "feel" for the relative weight value of the assets. It also helps the buyer and seller to negotiate the payment terms more realistically.

As to the payment terms in our example, the contract specifies as follows:

Cash down	$ 65,000
— assigned to the tangible assets	
Consulting contract	60,000
— payable $5,000 per mo	
(commencing July of year of sale)	
Secured promissory note	125,000
— payable over 5 yrs @ 8% p.a.	
(commencing after consulting contract)	
	$250,000

These terms constitute a *contingent installment sale*. The contingency is the completion of the one-year consulting contract by the seller. The inference is that by assigning the cash down amount to the tangible assets, and paying the seller for his continued expertise, the $125,000 promissory note could be negotiated later. If this is indeed contemplated, the contract should so state the possibility.

The Schedule F Sale

In the scenario above, the wife wasn't anxious to sell her horse-breeding business. But, because of her various IRS audits, she couldn't see any net profit potential over the next several years. She decided she'd have to sell, trade, or "do something." What she really wanted was some ranch land of her own.

So, before listing her business for sale, she shopped around for small parcels of land in rural areas accessible from her home. She found a suitable 10-acre parcel nestled in the foothills, but it had no public access. In other words, it was "landlocked." There was an oral easement for access with the neighbor, and, on this basis, the owner of the 10 acres wanted $150,000. The wife figured she could get the property for less than this amount through a like-kind exchange. She had seen deals like this advertised in her AQHA publications.

She got a rural real estate broker experienced in handling farm exchanges, and listed her business for sale. In due time, she received an offer from a more prosperous horse breeder that met her $165,000 price tag. The contract allocated the assets as follows:

		Amount	Fraction
1.	Stallion, registered	$ 75,000	0.4546
2.	Brood mares, 3: registered	60,000	0.3637
3.	Saddle gear & accessories	2,000	0.0121
4.	Corrals & equipment	5,000	0.0303
5.	Truck & 2 trailers	23,000	0.1393
		$165,000	1.0000

Note that this allocation shows tangible assets only. There are no customer lists, goodwill, or covenants. The buyer had his own intangibles and customers. The wife had no inventory, as she sold her last youngling before putting her business up for sale.

As to the payment terms, the sales contract specifies as follows:

Cash down	$ 30,000
10 Acres (approx) ranch land	135,000

(subject to exchange & obtaining
an easement contract for access)

$165,000

If you examine these terms, you'll see that the stallion and three brood mares (totaling $135,000) are being exchanged for 10 acres of ranch land. There is a question whether this arrangement qualifies as a "like-kind" (tax deferred) exchange. Nevertheless, we'll assume that it does qualify. Because of the uncertainty of getting a long-term easement contract, the terms of this sale constitute a *contingent like-kind exchange*. Also, because most farm-land owners rarely have $30,000 in cash, the broker must find a "third party" who wants the breeding business without any land.

Two Forms 8594 Required

Because two separate sales are involved — one by the husband and one by the wife — two separate Forms 8594 (Asset Acquisition Statements) are required. For distinguishing between the two proprietorship sales, we'll designate Form 8594(**H**) for husband and Form 8594(**W**) for wife. This or a similar designating distinction is necessary when married persons file their Form 1040 returns jointly. Each has his or her own individual Tax ID number which has to be tax-traced through, from the beginning of each business . . . to its end.

Also, recall that when an attorney, broker, or escrow agent closes a sale, a Form 1099-S (Gross Proceeds) is prepared and electronically transferred to the IRS. Obviously, the Tax ID of each spousal owner must be appropriately identified with his/her respective sale. Otherwise, you'd really gum up the IRS's computer-matching network. In Figure 9.1, we portray the importance of this Tax ID distinction.

Recall back in Figure 7.4 the general arrangement of Form 8594. There are three parts to the form, namely: Part I (General Information), Part II (Assets Transferred), and Part III (Supplemental Statement). In the case of Form 8594(H), there would be an entry in Part III, whereas there would be no such entry on Form 8594(W).

Part I of each Form 8594 would show the respective sale price of each business, namely: $250,000 for (H) and $165,000 for (W).

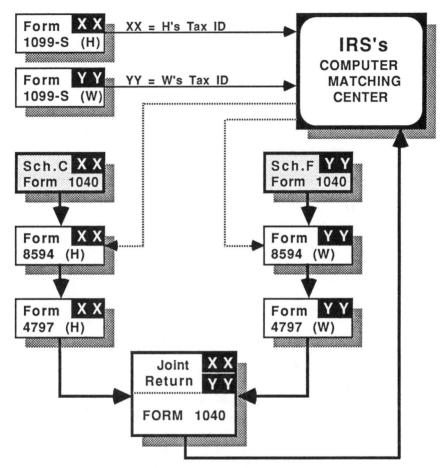

Fig. 9.1 - "ID Tracing" on a Joint (H&W) Return

As to Part II of each form, there would be no entries for Class I assets (cash and equivalents), nor for Class II (marketable securities). The asset Classes III and IV would appear as follows:

	8594(H)	8594(W)
Class III (tangibles)	$170,000	$165,000
Class IV (goodwill, etc.)	80,000	-0-
	$250,000	$165,000

For the Part II checkbox question about an ongoing arrangement between buyer and seller, Form 8594(H) would show a "Yes" ☒ and Form 8594 (W) would show a "No" ☒ . Then, the follow-on question is:

If "Yes," specify (a) the type of agreement, and (b) the maximum amount of consideration (not including interest) paid or to be paid under the agreement.

In the white space under Part II, the Form 8594(H) would show:

(a) Consulting contract: 1 year commencing July 1, 19___ and ending June 30, 19___ .
(b) $60,000 payable $5,000 per month (no interest).

Also in Part II, Form 8594(H) would list as Class IV:

Asset	Fair Market Value	Allocation of Sale Price
Fire Manual	$25,000 (5 yrs in the making)	$15,000
Customer List	$43,750 (35% of 3-yr average annual billings of $125,000)	$30,000

In Part II, it is always advisable to indicate computations of a market value that exceeds the amount allocated from the total sale price. This way, the IRS is less apt to assert that you are "skewing the books" to favor the buyer. Even so, for the two items listed, you'll have to justify the fair market values. Most likely, the fire manual would be technically obsolete after three years. Realistically, fires and fire customers are not likely to be repetitive for more than a few years at a time. Thus, adjustments in Part III may be required.

Also, Two Forms 4797

As described in Chapter 8, Form 4797: Sales of Business Property, is an intermediate step between Form 8594 and various entries on Form 1040. For this, you may wish to recall Figure 8.5.

Technically, once the asset allocation of sale price is made, both of our "scenario sales" could be put on one Form 4797. This is because the items sold are entered asset-by-asset, and not in bulk. BUT — there's the IRS with its paranoia for computer matching everything!

Do you know what would happen if you combined the two sale prices (gross proceeds) on Form 1099-S(H) and Form 1099-S(W), by entering $415,000 ($250,000 + $165,000) in the line 1 entry box on one Form 4797?

Answer: The IRS's computer would not be able to find the $250,000 under the husband's Tax ID, nor would it find the $165,000 under the wife's Tax ID. It's so "dumb" that it can't even add the two figures together to come up with the $415,000. So, what happens? Robotic automation is set in motion. The IRS sends out a proposed assessment on $250,000 of "unreported income" to the husband, and a separate proposed assessment on $165,000 of "unreported income" to the wife.

Obviously, the only computer-safe thing to do is to prepare **two** separate Forms 4797, namely: 4797(H) and 4797(W). Each form conspicuously displays in its entry Line 1 the separately broker reported amounts of $250,000 and $165,000. Recall from Figure 8.1 how we emphasized this particular item. We did so because "Box 1" is the only bulk sales information that the IRS computer sees. Also, recall from Figure 8.5 (on page 8-16) how Forms 1099-S and 8594 "come together" at Box 1 (of Form 4797).

With computer matching in mind, two Forms 4797 make sense in another respect. The 4797(H) can be matched up with the husband's Schedule C, with his own Tax ID. Similarly, the 4797(W) can be matched up with the wife's Schedule F, with her own Tax ID.

Before either Form 4797 can be started, Schedule C needs to be updated from January 1 to the closing date of sale. Similarly, Schedule F also needs to be updated. On each of these schedules there needs to be some notation that the business was sold. Inexplicably, neither Schedule C nor Schedule F has any checkbox inquiry or item for indicating such. Consequently, our suggestion is that along the right-hand vertical edging (in the white space), each proprietor hand prints the letters:

BUSINESS SOLD (date): See Form 4797

This way, hopefully, the IRS computer transcribers will see the notation and match up Schedule C with Form 4797(H) and Schedule F with Form 4797(W).

Cost Recovery Worksheet

Before tackling Form 4797, certain preparatory effort is required. This effort involves focusing on all depreciation and amortization deductions that have been taken against the assets sold, since date of acquisition. In other words, you have to resurrect all of your cost recovery deductions over the years and cumulatively total them up to the day before the date of sale. You need to do this for every asset or asset class that was listed in your contract of sale. For this, you need to prepare a cost recovery worksheet.

A sample of the kind of worksheet data we have in mind is presented in Figure 9.2. The idea here is to have an organized backup to all of the columnar information that is entered into Form 4797. Most of this information should be at your fingertips via your regularly maintained depreciation and amortization schedules. But, if not, you will have to dig back through your various records (invoices particularly) and tax returns which show the assets when you first placed them in service. You'll then have to reconstruct the cumulative depreciation/amortization that you have taken (cost recovered) over the years. The total cumulative amount is shown as item 15 in Figure 9.2. The amount at item 17 is a summation of the three bold-asterisked items highlighted in the figure.

Most of the entry items listed in Figure 9.2, we believe, are self-explanatory. But one item, namely: *Section 179 deduction*, requires additional explanation. In the tax code, this section is titled: *Election to Expense Certain Depreciable Business Assets*. Prior to 1997, an owner could one-time expense up to $17,500 of purchased equipment in the year of placement in service, instead of depreciating it. Acquisitions after 1996 can be expensed up to $25,000. This section is a concession to the small business owner that allows him to tax-recoup some of his asset costs upfront, without waiting years and years to do so. It is a "per year" election applicable only to equipment purchased in the year of the election.

To qualify for the Section 179 election, the equipment must be "acquired by purchase" and must be "tangible depreciable property" other than real estate. The item acquired must be used in the "active conduct" of a trade or business — **any** trade or business (manufacturing, farming, mining, selling, consulting, etc.). The items

COST RECOVERY WORKSHEET	Cumulative Depreciation and Amortization		
Item	Asset #1	Asset #2	Asset #3
1 Description of property			
2 Date placed in service			
3 Date improved			
4 Initial cost or basis ★	$	$	$
5 Cost of improvements ★	$	$	$
6 Adjusted cost: Item 4 plus Item 5			
7 Section 179 deduction			
8 Other applicable code sections			
9 Cumulative recovery, prior years (excluding Sec. 179)			
10 Basis for depreciation or amortization			
11 Method or convention used			
12 Recovery period: years			
13 Rate or table %			
14 Current years recovery			
15 TOTAL cumulative recovery: Items 7, 9, and 14			
16 Allocable expense of sale ★	$	$	$
17 TOTAL Cost + Improvements + Expense of Sale			

Fig. 9.2 - Information Needed for Preparing Form 4797

acquired may be machinery, tools, vehicles, equipment, storage facilities, agricultural structures, breedstock animals, mining shafts, etc. There must be an ongoing productive enterprise, in contrast to passive activities such as property rentals and general investments.

If the Section 179 election is used, any remaining unrecovered cost of the item purchased must be depreciated under the applicable class life rules. This explains the need in Figure 9.2 for a separate line entry: *Basis for depreciation or amortization.* For example, suppose you bought a $25,000 item of business equipment. If you elected to expense $15,000 of that amount, the remaining $10,000 would have to be depreciated. Be aware that the Section 179 election does not apply to amortizable intangibles.

The effort implied in Figure 9.2 seems like a lot of reconstructive work. And it is! After a few years in business, most proprietors tend to get careless about the historical importance of their asset costs. They get preoccupied with day-to-day affairs to the point where they do not concern themselves with the information needed when the business is sold.

"Expense of Sale" Allocations

Previously, we have stressed the importance of allocating proportionately the sale price of the business to each asset or class of assets being sold. This is a fundamental requirement before making any property-sold entry on Form 4797. Column (a) of the form asks for "description of property," and column (d) asks for "gross sale price." For each asset sold, the "gross sale price" is the *allocable portion* of the total sale price . . . **without** any offsets whatsoever.

Similarly, allocationwise, column (f) on Form 4797 asks for: "Cost or other basis, plus improvements, and *expense of sale.*" It is the expense-of-sale portion that we now address. Just as the sale price is allocated, so must the expense of sale be allocated.

Typically, in a commercial sale, the commission paid by the seller to the brokerage firm (or firms) handling the deal is 10% of the sale price. To this amount, there is added the expense of closing, title costs, state sales tax (as applicable), and other related expenses paid outside of escrow. Altogether, these selling expenses amount to 12% or more of the total sale price of the business. There is no mandatory reporting of these expenses to the IRS, as there is in the case of the gross proceeds. Nor will the IRS allow the reporting broker to discount (or offset) the gross proceeds with the known-in-escrow selling expenses. This means that it is up to each seller to identify, document, and claim on his return, all of the actual expenses of the sale.

In each of our scenario sales above, we computed and listed the allocation fraction of each asset sold. The same fraction applies also to the 12% or so of the expenses necessary to close the sale. For example, in our $250,000 Schedule C sale, the expenses for the sale would be $30,000 ($250,000 x 12%). This amount is "spread over" all of the assets sold as follows:

Asset sold	Fraction of sale price	Allocable expense of sale
1. Truck & accessories	0.1400	$ 4,200
2. Fire tools & instruments	0.1000	3,000
3. Office furniture & equip.	0.0200	600
4. Copyrighted fire manual	0.0600	1,800
5. Customer list	0.1200	3,600
6. Consulting contract	0.2400	7,200
7. Goodwill, etc.	0.3200	9,600
Totals	1.0000	$30,000

This same expense-of-sale allocation procedure is used for the Schedule F scenario sale.

Because we knew that the allocable expense-of-sale information would be needed when preparing Form 4797, we provided a separate entry line for this in Figure 9.2. We also provided a separate entry line for recording the "cost of improvements," if any, to each asset prior to sale. All too often, these costs are expensed as "repairs and maintenance," where they become lost in the bookkeeping jungle.

Now, Form 4797(H)

At this point, we should be ready to make our first entries onto Form 4797(H). The "(H)", recall, is the husband proprietor who sold his Schedule C business.

Of the seven items previously listed as being sold by the husband, the first three (truck, tools, and furniture) are clearly depreciable trade or business property. As such, all three items are subject separately to the Section 1245 recapture rules. This means that these items are first entered in Part III of Form 4797. We'll tell you now that each of the three items was sold at a gain. Part III, recall, applies only to the *gain* from disposition of property under Sections 1245, etc.

For illustrative purposes, we present in Figure 9.3 the necessary calculations for completing Part III of Form 4797(H). We have edited and simplified the arrangement so that you can glean the basic substance involved. The portion of the total sale price of the business affected by Part III is $65,000.

The net result of Figure 9.3 is that $5,800 of the total gain enters onto Part I of Form 4797(H); $37,900 enters onto Part II. Because

Sec. 1245 Property: Recapture Computations				
Description of Gain Property Held More Than 1 Year				
● Office Furniture & Equipment ● Fire Tools & Instruments ● Truck & Access				Totals
1. Gross sale price $	35,000	25,000	5,000	65,000
2. Cost plus improvements plus expense of sale	29,200	28,000	5,600	
3. Depreciation allowed since acquisition	20,000	18,000	3,500	
4. Adjusted basis - Subtract step 3 from step 2	9,200	10,000	2,100	
5. GAIN Realized - Subtract step 4 from step 1	25,800	15,000	2,900	43,700
Recapture Amounts				
6. Depreciation allowed	20,000	18,000	3,500	
7. Enter SMALLER of step 5 or step 6	20,000	15,000	2,900	37,900
x. Total gain for all properties				43,700
y. Total of step 7: ENTER in Part II				37,900
z. Subtract y from x: ENTER in Part I				5,800

Fig. 9.3 - Text Example of Part III of Form 4797(H)

of the way we intentionally chose our example, nothing else numerically enters onto the form. But there are two other parts of the sale still unaccounted for. These are the $60,000 consulting contract and the $125,000 installment note for the intangibles. We have to account (in the year of sale) for the full $250,000 sale price of the business.

As to the 1-year $5,000-per-month consulting contract, the seller has to start a **new** Schedule C. This is because "consulting" is a *personal service* activity even though it lasts for only one year. Consequently, Schedule C — NOT Form 4797 — applies. Since only six months of personal service was rendered in the year of sale, the gross receipts on the Schedule C become $30,000. Because this is one-half of the consulting contract, 50% of the allocable $7,200 expense of sale ($3,600) is entered on Schedule C as an item of "other expense." There may be other consulting expenses that can be claimed before paying self-employment tax on the net Schedule C earnings.

What about the $125,000 installment note for the intangibles (copyright, customer list, and goodwill)? Since there would be no payment on these items until after the consulting contract was completed, there is no gain or loss to enter on Form 4797. HOWEVER, the installment contract still has to be year-of-sale reported. How is this done?

Answer: By using Form 6252: *Installment Sale Income*, and blending it into Form 4797 as an indirect entry, as indicated back in Figure 8.3. This installment form prescribes a separate set of calculations which is repeated each year that any payment on principal is received. The year-of-sale computation produces a Gross Profit Ratio (GPR = gross profit ÷ gross sale price) which is applied to the amount of principal received each year. For example, assume a GPR of 0.88 and a payment on principal of $25,000. The taxable amount to be entered on Form 4797 would be $22,000 ($25,000 x 0.88). We'll explain the computational sequence in more detail in Chapter 12.

And Now, Form 4797(W)

The Schedule F sale for the wife as a proprietor was a two-part sale. As you recall earlier, there was a $30,000 cash part and a $135,000 exchange part.

The $30,000 cash part was expressly for reimbursing the seller for her equipment-type assets: truck, trailers, corrals, and saddle gear. As a class group, she paid $50,000 for these items and had cost recovered (depreciated) only $20,000 at time of sale. The effect was that she was paid her net book value. Nevertheless, she has a Form 4797(W) **loss** to the extent of the allocable share of her selling expenses, namely: $3,600 ($30,000 x 12% expense of sale). All of these assets were held for more than one year.

It is tempting to consider the $30,000 cash part as one asset grouping, and make a single entry in Part I of Form 4797(W). But, because the three items were carried on her depreciation schedules separately — and correctly so — she must enter them separately in Part I. Upon doing this, the pertinent results would be:

	Sale price	Depreciation allowed	Cost plus expense	LOSS
1. Truck & 2 trailers	$23,000	15,000	40,760	2,760
2. Corrals & equip.	5,000	4,000	9,600	600
3. Saddle gear, etc.	2,000	1,000	3,240	240
Totals	$30,000	20,000	53,600	<$3,600>

If there were no other gains or losses in Part I, the <$3,600> loss would drop down to Part II to become an ordinary loss (rather than a capital loss).

As to the $135,000 exchange part of the sale, we have to acquaint you with another required form. This is Form 8824: *Like-Kind Exchanges*. It accepts those exchange arrangements where both nonlike and like-kind properties are exchanged. Generally speaking, *no gain or loss* is tax recognized for exchanges of solely like-kind property. This was the case for our Schedule F scenario example. Accordingly, at the entry line in Part I of Form 4797(W) identified as: *Gain/Loss from Form 8824*, you should enter either "Zero" or "-0-". This tells the IRS that you are reporting the exchange part on Form 8824. This form must be attached to your return for the year of sale/exchange. We'll comment further on like-kind exchanges in Chapter 12.

Pulling Things Together

We have intentionally chosen a proprietorship as our first example sale, because it permits a general presentation of the tax fundamentals involved. Selling a business is not just something that you agonize over the terms of the sale, and then go about business as usual. The sale is an acutely interruptive factor. It forces you to think differently when preparing your Form 1040 for the year of sale.

By "thinking differently," we mean that you need to think in **three** distinct phases of tax accounting. There is Phase I which is all of your *pre-sale* accounting. There is Phase II which is all of your *sale* accounting. And there is Phase III which is all of your *post-sale* accounting. Each phase has to be done on its own; you can't blend them altogether as you normally would when doing your annual return.

The Phase I of your Form 1040 preparation is to bring forward all of your regular business income and expenses, up to the date of

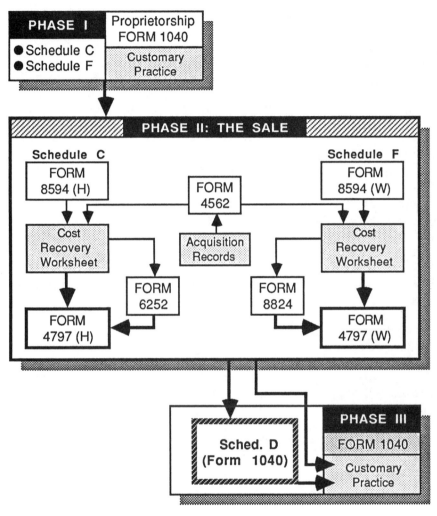

Fig. 9.4 - Return Preparation When Proprietorship Is Sold

sale of the business. In other words, you post and close out your Schedule C and/or Schedule F appropriately. None of the business sale information goes on these schedules. As we suggested earlier, you should indicate your close-out by hand printing on either or both schedules:

BUSINESS SOLD (date): See Form 4797

In other words, Phase I is a continuation of what you have been customarily doing in previous years, except that it is a "short year" accounting in the year your business is sold.

The Phase II of your return preparation is strictly a focus on the reporting of and the accounting for all assets sold: asset by asset. The target, of course, is Form 4797 with all of its associated worksheets and tax forms. You may recall that the "associated forms" are: (1) Form 1099-S: Gross Proceeds, (2) Form 8594: Asset Statement, (3) Form 6252: Installment Sale, and (4) Form 8824: Like Exchange. There is also Form 4562: Depreciation and Amortization, which has to be posted up to the date of sale as part of the Phase I effort. The information from Form 4562 and its backup records and worksheets constitutes the background for preparing the Cost Recovery Worksheet that we depicted in Figure 9.2. When all of the associated forms and worksheets are ready, then — and only then — can Form(s) 4797 be completed. The involvement here, and its interruptiveness between Phases I and III, is presented in Figure 9.4. As you can see, the Form(s) 4797 become the entire effort of focus in Phase II.

Phase III (post-sale) involves the transferring of information from Form(s) 4797 onto Form 1040. As was depicted back in Figure 8.5, there is an intermediate Schedule D: Capital Gains and Losses, to contend with. Not only does Schedule D (Form 1040) accept information from Part I of Form 4797, it also accommodates Forms 6252 (installment sales) and 8824 (exchanges). These latter forms may additionally be required when other assets are sold independently of the bulk sale of the business. Part II of Form 4797 goes directly onto page 1 of Form 1040, after which your return can be completed in your customary manner.

10

SALE OF PARTNERSHIP

> A Partnership Pays No Income Tax On Its Own. Instead, Each Partner Pays His/Her "Pro Rata Share" Of The Tax On His/Her Own Form 1040. When A Partnership Interest Is Sold Or Exchanged, It Is A CAPITAL ASSET, Except For Certain Section 751 "Unrealizables." If 50% Or More Interests Are Sold, The Partnership Must Terminate. Then, Full Allocation Of Its Multiple Assets Is Required. Numerous Adjustments To Books Of Account Are Required To Pinpoint Each Partner's Exact Ownership Percentage On Date Of Sale.

A partnership is a separate business entity distinct from the individual members thereof. As such, there is a partnership return to be filed — Form 1065 — with its own Tax ID number. Separately, there is a Schedule K-1 (Form 1065) for each member with his or her own Tax ID keyed directly to the partnership's ID. The spouses of partners are not themselves partners, unless they are active participants in the day-to-day affairs of the entity.

A partnership consists of two or more principals who are the owners —co-owners, actually — of the business. There is no statutory limit to the number of principals that can be involved, but five seems to be a practical limit. When there are more than five principals, ownership controversies arise and the business is pulled in different directions simultaneously. Invariably, some dissatisfied partner wants his "money out now." When this happens, the partnership is deprived of operating capital and the business soon takes a nosedive.

Every successful partnership has a *written* Partnership Agreement. This contract spells out the duties, responsibilities, contributions of capital, and the percent ownership of the business by each member. There is no requirement that all partners/principals share equally in the profits or losses of the business. Often this sharing is directly proportional to the ownership of capital in the business, assuming that all partners work equally hard to make the business successful. For example, the sharing could be 40% for Partner A, 35% for Partner B, and 25% for Partner C (40% + 35% + 25% = 100%). Even though the profit/loss sharing is unequal, all partners have an equal voice and voting power in the affairs of the business. When a partnership is sold, all partners must agree. However, any partner may sell his or her own interest at any time, independent of the other members of the entity.

In this chapter, we want to address the sale of a partnership strictly from the point of view of one partner selling his or her entire ownership interest. Whether one partner sells, and no others do; or whether two partners sell; or whether they all sell — individually or simultaneously — the procedural aspects and tax accounting requirements are the same. In this regard, it is helpful to think of a partnership as a loose association of individuals, each of whom is a sole proprietor.

Introduction to Form 1065

If you've been in a partnership previously, or are currently in one, you probably already know what Form 1065 is. But, chances are, you will not know of its reporting features at time of sale of a portion or all of the business. Similarly to a proprietorship, there is a pre-sale operating phase which continues — with significant adjustments — after one partner terminates his interest by sale or exchange. Relative to this pre-sale phase, we briefly want to refresh your knowledge of certain contents of Form 1065.

In Figure 10.1, we present a highly abbreviated arrangement of Form 1065: *Partnership Return of Income*. As you can see, it has a head portion, an income portion, a deduction portion, a cost of goods sold portion, an "other information" portion, and a signature portion. In its "short" version, Form 1065 consists of two full pages, front and back. There are other schedules and forms that attach to Form 1065, particularly a Schedule K-1 for each partner.

FORM 1065	PARTNERSHIP RETURN OF INCOME		Year

A	Principal Business	Partnership's Name & Address	D	Tax ID
B	Product or Service		E	Date Started
C	Code Number		F	Total Assets
G	Type of Return	☐ Initial ☐ Final ☐ Amended ☐ Change of Address		
H	Method	☐ Cash ☐ Accrual ☐ Other _____		
I	▶▶▶▶▶ Number of Partners ▶ _____			

INCOME PORTION
DEDUCTIONS PORTION

Schedule A	COST OF GOODS SOLD
Schedule B	OTHER INFORMATION

Designation of Tax Matters Partner

SIGNATURE BLOCK

/s/ General Partner _____   _____ date _____

/s/ Paid Preparer _____   _____ date & ID _____

Fig. 10.1 - Abbreviated Contents of Partnership Form 1065

The income, deductions, and cost-of-goods-sold portions on Form 1065 are similar to any other business tax return that you have seen or have prepared. Schedule C (Form 1040): Profit or Loss from Business, is a good example. The term "cost of goods sold," however, does NOT include the sale of the proprietorship business itself, or of a partner's separate interest.

The "other information" portion of Form 1065 consists of some 15 specific questions which must be answered ☐ Yes or ☐ No. The purpose of these questions is to establish the character of the business. Is it a limited partnership, a tax shelter, a publicly traded partnership, an affiliate of a foreign entity, or does it have assets less than $250,000? Most of the questions should be answered "No." Our premise is that your entity is a general partnership carrying on a bona fide trade or business that is the main source of livelihood for each of the principals involved.

The last three questions do require specific attention. In edited form, these questions are:

1. Was there a distribution of property or a transfer of a partnership interest during the tax year? ☐ Yes ☐ No
2. Was the partnership in operation at the end of the tax year? ☐ Yes ☐ No
3. How many months during the tax year was the partnership actively operated? ▶ _____

These questions are obviously intended to alert the IRS and its computer processors to the occurrence of any sale that substantially affects the "going concern value" of the partnership business.

A "Pass-Through" Entity

A partnership as an entity is not subject to tax. Any liability for tax passes through to each individual partner. Section 701 of the tax code makes this very clear:

A partnership as such shall not be subject to the income tax imposed [herein]. *Persons **carrying on business** as partners shall be liable for income tax only in their separate or individual capacities.* [Emphasis added.]

The phrase "carrying on business" requires that there be some principal or core activity in which each partner actively participates on a day-to-day basis. The result is an activity in which each partner, as a part-owner, is self-employed therein. No regular salaries or wages are paid. Instead, each owner gets his (or her) "distributive share" of the net earnings at the end of each tax accounting period.

The means by which each partner's distributive share is passed through is Schedule K-1 (Form 1065). This document is officially titled: ***Partner's Share of Income, Credits, Deductions, Etc.*** It is prepared by the partnership at the end of its accounting year, or whenever a partner terminates his interest in the partnership. The dollar-entry contents represent each partner's share of the partnership activities. The original of each K-1 is attached to the partnership's Form 1065 and forwarded to the IRS as required. A copy is sent to each partner for his or her own records.

In the headportion of the Schedule K-1, each partner's percentage of the business is indicated as follows:

	(i) Before change or termination	(ii) End of year
(a) Profit sharing	_____ %	_____ %
(b) Loss sharing	_____ %	_____ %
(c) Ownership of capital	_____ %	_____ %

In most cases, the three percentages are the same. However, if the partnership agreement indicates otherwise, the profit or loss percentages may differ from the ownership percentage. Each partner's share of liabilities is indicated as:

(a) Nonrecourse debt	$_____
(b) Qualified real estate financing	$_____
(c) Other enforceable debt	$_____

The accompanying instructions to the K-1 tell each partner to—

Use the total of the three liability amounts for computing the adjusted basis of your partnership interest.

This is another one of those reminders that you cannot just sell your partnership interest and walk away from your share of its liabilities.

Partners' Capital Accounts

A partnership operates the way it does because the partners, as individuals, contribute capital in the form of cash and/or property. When property is contributed, its fair market value becomes the partner's contributory amount. The contribution of each partner may vary during the year, depending on the self-discipline of each in meeting his/her capital obligations under the partnership agreement. There also may be variations between the beginning of a year and the end of a year, due to operational increases, decreases, adjustments, and distributions.

To keep track of these affairs, separate books of account are required called: *Partners' Capital Accounts.* There is a separate subaccount for Partner A, a separate subaccount for Partner B, a separate subaccount for Partner C . . . and so on. This is a tax requirement pursuant to Section 704: *Partner's Distributive Share*. Subsection 704(b) is particularly pertinent here. This subsection: Determination of Distributive Share, reads in part—

A partner's distributive share of income, gain, loss, deduction, or credit (or item thereof) shall be determined in accordance with the partner's interest in the partnership (determined by taking into account all facts and circumstances), if— [Emphasis added.]

Each partnership has its own system for keeping track of all "facts and circumstances" surrounding each partner's capital interest. Even so, each system must include the following essential elements:

1. Capital account at beginning of year   _____
2. Capital contributed during the year   _____
3. Allocable net income or loss per books   _____
4. Other increases (itemize)   _____
5. Withdrawals and distributions   _____
6. Other decreases (itemize)   _____
7. Capital account at end of year   _____

These and other partners' capital accounting requirements are set forth in approximately 65,000 words of regulations, commencing with Reg. 1.704-1: Partner's distributive share.

In essence, all of the regulatory wording boils down to the fact that each partner's "distributive share" in the business is—

$$\frac{\text{His average daily capital account for the year}}{\text{Total average daily capital accounts for all partners}}$$

This gives a percentage figure, such as 36.82%. This is treated as the partner's ownership interest in the business, unless the partnership agreement specifies otherwise.

Note that we use the phrase: "average **daily** capital account." If a partner puts up $1,000 at the beginning of the year, and $11,000 the last day of the year, he would have a $12,000 end-of-the-year capital account. Right? But his average daily capital account would be only $1,034 ($1,000 x 364 days + $12,000 x 1 day ÷ 365 days). It's almost like a daily bank accounting system. Obviously, the partner or partners who keep their capital in throughout the year deserve a higher allocable share of the business than the partner or partners who put money in, take it out, and put it back in at the very end of the year. This fine point in capital accounting becomes a very important issue when a partner's interest in the business is sold.

Ordinary Course of Events

Because a general partnership is an agreement between self-employed individuals, two distinct functional roles emerge. There is the *ordinary course* of trade or business role, called: the **nonpassive** role. There is a "nonordinary" role called the *passive* role. This distinction is important because there are very stringent loss limitation rules for passive activities in a partnership [IRC Sec. 469]. It is the nonpassive role on which we focus when selling a partnership interest in the business. Always keep in mind that a buyer of any business wants an entity which has determinable "going concern" value. Passive partnerships tend to be loss entities (for tax sheltering) which very few buyers want.

In the normal course of operations, each partner prepares his own Form 1040 based on the Schedule K-1 information he receives from the partnership. The K-1 is **not** attached to the partner's Form 1040. Instead, information from the K-1 goes onto various schedules and forms which themselves attach to a partner's Form 1040. This is the consequence of the "pass through" feature of all partnerships.

As depicted in Figure 10.2, the most significant attachment to a partner's Form 1040 is Schedule E, Part II. The Schedule E is titled: **Supplemental Income and Loss**. The Part II is titled: *Income or Loss from Partnerships*. This is where you start entering the information reported to you on Schedule K-1 onto your Form 1040. Schedule E, Part II requires that the name of the partnership be entered along with *its* Tax ID number.

Altogether, the main body of a Schedule K-1 consists of approximately 50 lines for entering distributive share information about the partnership. Ordinarily, no more than about 5 to 10 of these entry lines are used during a normal operating year. Each entry has to be accurately fractioned for each partner's own capital interest (pro rata) in the partnership. Consequently, a lot of "dog work" accounting is required when preparing the K-1s.

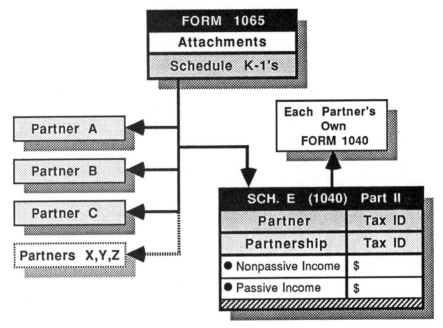

Fig. 10.2 - The Pass-Through Aspects of a Partnership Business

When a partner sells or exchanges (terminates) his partnership interest during an operating year, a **short-year** K-1 has to be prepared. It is issued only for that partner, if his ownership interest is less than 50%. This can — and often does — cause a major disruption to the accounting process of the partnership as a whole. There is much added expense for this short-year K-1 preparation.

Sale or Exchange Treatment

A partner's (capital account) interest in a partnership is treated as a capital asset, in and of itself. There is one exception which you'll see shortly. But, otherwise, a partner's ownership share is treated almost like stock in a corporation. Not really, but "almost." This is the gist of Section 741: *Recognition and Character of Gain or Loss on Sale or Exchange.* This section reads in full as—

*In the case of a sale or exchange of an interest in a partnership, gain or loss shall be recognized to the **transferor partner**. Such gain or loss shall be considered as gain or loss from the* *sale or exchange of a **capital asset**, except as otherwise provided in section 751 (relating to unrealized receivables and inventory items which have appreciated substantially in value).* [Emphasis added.]

Except to the extent that Section 751 applies, a partner — called: "transferor" — who sells or exchanges his interest in the partnership experiences capital gain or loss therewith. The amount of gain or loss is determined by the difference between the amount realized (gross sale price) and the adjusted basis of the partner's interest. A partner's "adjusted basis" is essentially his capital account on the date of sale. It would be his capital account if he contributed all cash and no property to the partnership, and if he had no indebtedness which the partnership assumed, and if there were no other partnership liabilities.

If property is contributed, the contributing partner's tax basis in that property is used to establish his adjusted capital basis. This is so, even though he was credited with the fair market value of the property when capital accounting for his ownership interest.

For example, consider that a partner has a $100,000 capital account which consists of $10,000 in cash and $90,000 in market value of property. The property could be real estate, machinery and equipment, marketable securities, inventory, or whatever. Suppose the contributor's tax basis in that property was only $30,000. (He paid $65,000 for it but deducted $35,000 in depreciation allowances before becoming a member of the partnership.) His adjusted capital basis on the date of sale would be $40,000 ($10,000 cash plus $30,000 property basis): NOT $100,000.

Keep in mind that the adjusted basis in a partner's interest is a tax reference only. It is a necessary element for determining the partner's capital gain or capital loss at time of sale (or exchange) of his individual interest. The concept is similar to that of acquiring stock in a corporation where one's tax basis and market value are different. The rules for tax basis accounting are found in Section 705: *Determination of Basis of Partner's Interest.* As a result of this "basis business," two parallel capital accounts have to be maintained for each partner. One subaccount is labeled: *Tax*, for tax basis purposes; the parallel subaccount is labeled: *Book*, for distributive share purposes. During ordinary course of operations, the distributive share account is used. But, at time of sale or exchange, the *tax basis* account is used.

Exception to the Above

In the capital gain/loss treatment in Section 741 above, there is mention of the Section 751 exception. This exception is one of those recapture-type rules intended to prevent the "skewing" of books that would convert otherwise ordinary income into capital gain. Its effect is similar to that which we discussed in Chapter 8 with respect to Section 1231 (capital gain/ordinary loss) and Form 4797 (sales of business property).

Section 751 is titled: *Unrealized Receivables and Inventory Items*. Its subsection (a): Sale or Exchange of Interest in Partnership, is particularly pertinent. This subsection reads:

*The amount of any money, or the fair market value of any property, received by a **transferor partner** in exchange for all or part of his interest in the partnership attributable to—*
(1)   unrealized receivables of the partnership, or
(2)   inventory items of the partnership,
*shall be considered as an amount realized from the sale or exchange of property **other than** a capital asset.* [Emphasis added.]

The term "unrealized receivables" pertains to partnership rights to payment for goods delivered or to be delivered, or for services rendered or to be rendered [IRC Sec. 751(c)]. These are payments due that have not been entered on the partnership books as income, at the time a partner's interest is sold. The term also includes Sections 1245 and 1250 depreciation recapture on applicable partnership property.

The term "inventory items" applies to any inventory of goods and merchandise — and other noncapital assets — which are available for sale in the ordinary course of business [IRC Sec. 751(d)]. Typically, these items are carried on the partnership's books at their wholesale value. When sold to customers at retail, there is an "appreciation factor" that has to be considered when allocating a Section 751 amount to a selling partner.

In other words, when a partner sells or exchanges his ownership interest, he must first subtract from his gross proceeds an amount attributable to the Section 751 assets. The residual amount of the gross proceeds is then attributable to Section 741. The effect is as though the transferor partner, using Form 4797, enters his Section 751 transactions into Part II (Ordinary gains and losses) and his

Section 741 transactions into Part I (Capital gains and losses). Thus, only two classes of assets are being sold. He is not selling a "bundle of assets" as in the case of a proprietorship. We emphasize this point in Figure 10.3.

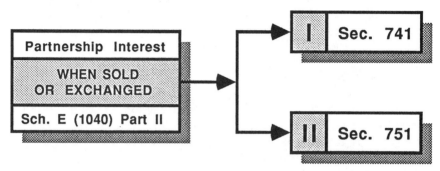

Fig. 10.3 - The "Two Asset" Feature of a Partnership Interest

Section 741 Analyzed

If you get nothing else out of this chapter, we want you to comprehend the significance of Section 741 and what it can do for you. Its title — again — is: *Recognition and Character of Gain or Loss on Sale or Exchange* . . . of a partnership interest. This is a "stand alone" section of the tax code. Various courts have held that it operates independently of other provisions that qualify capital assets. In fact, some 40 Tax Court and Federal Court of Appeals rulings have held that—

The sale of a partnership interest as an entity in itself, is a capital asset.

As far back as 1959, the IRS came out with Revenue Ruling 59-109, 1959-1 CB 168 stating that:

The sale of a partnership interest constitutes the sale of a capital asset, except with respect to unrealized receivables and inventory items which have appreciated substantially in value.

Reiterating what we have already mentioned, when you sell a partnership interest you are selling two classes of assets only. These are: (1) Section 741 (capital) assets, and (2) Section 751 (ordinary) assets. This means that Section 741 property includes **everything not included in** Section 751. Section 741 includes not only your ownership share of the tangible assets of the partnership, it includes your share of intangibles as well. That is, goodwill, covenant not to compete, customer lists, copyrights, patents, franchises — the whole works — are included. You don't have to segregate asset-by-asset and compute the gain or loss separately for each one.

Must Notify the Partnership

Every individual partner can sell his share of the partnership entity any time he wants to. This is a given. But ordinary business courtesy, if not the partnership agreement itself, requires that the selling (transferor) partner notify the partnership of his intentions and the status of his negotiations. Technically, if not legally, the transferor partner needs the "advice and consent" of the other partners before the sale can be finalized.

Proper notification affords other members of the partnership the opportunity to buy, or not to buy, the transferor's interest. Furthermore, any outside buyer wants assurance that the remaining partners approve of the sale, and that they will not set up any roadblocks to it.

Generally speaking, notification to the partnership must be given — *in writing* — no less than 30 days before the target date for closing the transferor's sale. Preferably, more than 30 days' notice should be given. This is because there are formidable accounting tasks to be performed by the partnership. The total assets of the partnership have to be re-examined and brought up to the target date. These total assets have to be percentage allocated between Section 741 property and Section 751 items. These Section 741/751 allocations have to be re-allocated among the members of the entity in proportion to each partner's ownership therein. Even without acrimony and disagreement among the partners, the Section 741/751 allocations are a tedious task. Perhaps you can appreciate this task better, after glancing at Figure 10.4.

If only one partner sells his interest to an outsider, and that interest represents less than 50% of the total partnership interest, the partnership *shall continue* [IRC Sec. 708(a)]. However, if one or more partners whose combined interests total 50% or more sell their interest to outsiders, the partnership *shall terminate* [IRC Sec. 708(b)].

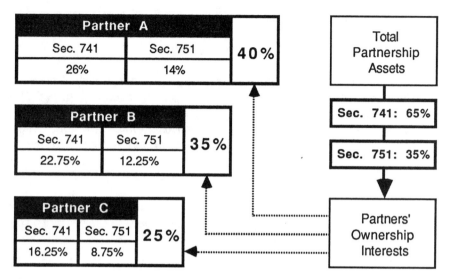

Fig. 10.4 - Example Ownership Allocation of Partnership Assets

Inconsistent Treatment Rule

As a full-year partner, the information on your K-1 should exact-match that which the IRS finds reported on your regular 1040. But when you sell or exchange your partnership interest, a divergence between the K-1 reportings and your reportings will most likely occur. This is because the partnership has to clear its books on a short-year basis, whereas you have to clear your books on a long-term basis. Over a period of 3, 5, or more years of active participation in the partnership business, your records and the partnership records would rarely be the same. When differences occur, you enter the tax world classed as: *Inconsistent Treatment*.

As a transferor/terminating partner, there are at least three areas where substantial differences could occur. These are—

One. Your exact ownership percentage on the date of sale.

Two. Your adjusted tax basis in your ownership interest.

Three. Your share of the Section 751 unrealizables.

And, due to the invariable frustrations of short-year accounting, other errors and inconsistencies will crop up between what you report and what the partnership reports.

In the official instructions accompanying Schedule K-1 (Form 1065), there is a section headed: Inconsistent Treatment of Items. In more succinct terms, the instruction says—

If the treatment on your original or amended return is inconsistent with the partnership's treatment, or **if the partnership** *was required to but* **has not filed a return,** *you* **must file** *Form 8082: Notice of Inconsistent Treatment.* [You must do so] *with your original or amended return* **to identify and explain** *any inconsistency (or to note that a partnership return has not been filed).* [Emphasis added.]

Our bet is that, upon the sale of your partnership interest, your short-year K-1 will **not** be received by the time you are ready to file your Form 1040. We also bet that, when you do receive it, there *will be* errors and inconsistencies. This is where Form 8082 really proves its worth.

Form 8082 permits you to describe and explain each item that you claim is inconsistent. It affords you the opportunity to put your characterization on a transaction, before the partnership gets around to it.

You have probably never heard of Form 8082 before. Ordinarily, as a full-year partner year after year, it would not come to your attention. But, when it comes time to sell your partnership interest, you will need it! Send a copy to the partnership, as well as to the IRS.

Section 751 Statement Required

As previously stated, when selling a partnership interest, there are only two classes of assets involved, namely: Section 741 (capital) and Section 751 (ordinary). It is the Section 751 category of assets that gets priority regulatory attention. Particularly on point are Regulations 1.751-1(a)(2) and 1.751-1(a)(3).

Regulation 1.751-1(a)(2): *Determination of gain or loss,* starts out by saying that—

The income or loss realized by a partner upon the sale or exchange of his interest in section 751 property is the difference between (i) **the portion** *of the total amount realized for the partnership interest* **allocated to section 751 property,** *and (ii) the portion of the selling partner's basis for his entire interest* *allocated to such property. Generally, the portion of the total amount realized which the seller and the purchaser allocate to section 751 property in **an arm's length agreement** will be regarded as correct.* [Emphasis added.]

The idea here is that the first cut-from-the-top of the gross proceeds of a sale is an amount attributable to "Section 751 property."

Regulation 1.751-1(a)(3) supports the above by requiring that a separate statement be attached to the selling partner's tax return. Excerpted portions of this regulation read—

*A transferor partner selling . . . his interest in a partnership which has **any** section 751 property at the time of the sale . . . **shall submit with his income tax return** . . . a statement setting forth separately the following information:*

*(i) The date of the sale, the amount of the transferor partner's **adjusted basis** for his partnership interest, and the portion thereof attributable to Section 751 property;*
(ii) The amount of any money and the fair market value of any other property received or to be received for the transferred interest in the partnership, and the portion thereof attributable to section 751 property. [Emphasis added.]

Reporting on Form 1040

How does the selling partner report the sale of his partnership interest on Form 1040?

Answer: He starts with Schedule E, Part II and, immediately below the line on which he enters the name of the partnership and its Tax ID, he inserts the hand-printed notation:

PARTNERSHIP INTEREST SOLD ON _____
See Form 4797 with Section 751 Statement Attached

If the "he" or "she" is you, and you have received a short-year K-1 by the time you are ready to file your 1040, enter the information from the K-1 first. In some cases, there may be K-1 entries that go on Form 4797 (Sales of Business Property) and/or on Schedule D (Capital Gains and Losses). In this regard, the Form

1040 preparatory situation is very analogous to reporting the sale of a proprietorship.

The Section 751 attachment to Form 4797 should not only comply with Regulation 1.751-1(a)(3); it should also include the computational aspects involved.

For example, you can use Form 8594 (Asset Acquisition Statement) to establish the amount of total sale price that is allocated to Section 751 property. You might enter a notation such as—

"On ___(date)___, the partnership was contacted for an allocable Section 751 amount, whereupon an estimate of $35,000 was furnished. The buyer agreed to this amount and paid cash to this extent in the total sale price of $165,000."

Then enter $35,000 in the sale price column of Part II (Ordinary Gains and Losses) of Form 4797. In column (a) for description of property enter "Section 751." The remainder amount of $130,000 (165,000 - 35,000) is entered in the sale price column in Part I (Capital Gains and Losses). In its description column, enter "Section 741." Figure 10.5 should be helpful in visualizing the action required on your part.

For the cost basis columns in Parts I and II of Form 4797, you have to allocate your total adjusted tax basis in the partnership . . . plus your selling expenses. Assume, for illustration purposes, that your total tax basis is $85,000 after adjustments for your share of the partnership liabilities. Accordingly, you compute your cost basis allocation as:

$$\text{Part I: } \$85,000 \times \frac{130}{165} = \$66,963$$

$$\text{Part II: } \$85,000 \times \frac{35}{165} = \underline{\$18,027}$$
$$\$85,000$$

In the depreciation "allowed or allowable" columns in Parts I and II, you enter zero (-0-). Do **not** leave these columns blank. If you do, the IRS will "impute" some entry amount based on other unrelated depreciation information on your return, or on the K-1.

If your dates acquired and sold are correct, you should wind up with a capital gain of $63,037 (130,000 - 66,963) in Part I, and an

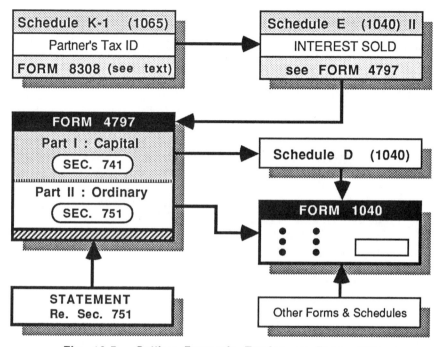

Fig. 10.5 - Selling Partner's Entries on Form 4797

ordinary gain of $16,973 (35,000 - 18,027) in Part II. You then follow the instructions on Form 4797 as an *individual*: NOT as a partnership.

If the partnership as an *entity* is sold or exchanged, Forms 8594 and 4797 are prepared by the partnership before any K-1s are issued.

Special Reporting: Form 8308

When a partner sells his interest in a partnership, a special tax information report is required. This is Form 8308: ***Report of Sale or Exchange of Certain Partnership Interests.*** Here, the term "certain" applies to those transactions where any part of the gross proceeds received is attributable to Section 751 property.

The 8308 report is prepared by the partnership and forwarded to the IRS. One copy is furnished to the transferor (the seller); a duplicate copy is furnished to the transferee (the buyer).

Form 8308 is **in addition to** any and all other information reports to the IRS by brokers and escrow agents, such as Form 1099-B (Proceeds from Broker Transactions), Form 1099-S (Proceeds from Real Estate Transactions), or Form 8594 (Asset Acquisition Statement). A separate Form 8308 is required for each partner whose interest is sold or exchanged.

When does the partnership file Form 8308? The instructions (on the form) say—

A partnership must file Form 8308 once it has notice of a section 751 transfer. The partnership has such notice when either:

(1) the partnership receives written notification of the sale or exchange from the transferor . . . ; or
(2) the partnership has knowledge that there has been a transfer of a partnership interest . . .

The partnership files Form 8308 by attaching it to its regular Form 1065 filed at the end of its accounting year. Or, the partnership may file it separately — within 30 days of notification of the sale — if it is anticipated that Form 1065 will be unavoidably late due to reasonable cause.

Like a Schedule K-1, a recipient partner does not need to file Form 8308 with his Form 1040. Not only does the IRS have the date of sale on its computer, it is standing ready to snare the transferor's Section 751 Statement that is a required attachment to the selling partner's tax return.

11

SALE OF CORPORATION

There Are Four Basic Ways Of Selling A Corporation: Sell The Assets, Sell The Stock, Redeem The Stock, Exchange The Stock . . . Or Combination Thereof. If Aggressive Public Offerings Are Made, There Is Risk Of Being Labeled A "Dealer In Securities" Rather Than A Seller Of A Business. Since Corporation Stock Is A CAPITAL ASSET Of Its Own, Its Sale — If Properly Tax Structured — Can Result In Capital Gain Treatment Rather Than Ordinary Dividend Treatment. In All Cases Herein, We Address Only SMALL Business Corporations . . . And Their Individual Shareholders.

Unlike a partnership, a corporation is a separate taxable entity of its own. It reports income and claims deductions and credits like any other trade or business. When there is net positive income, corporate tax rates apply. These are separate and apart from individual tax rates. A corporation gets no tax deductions for the dividends that it pays to its shareholders. As such, the dividends are taxed at each shareholder's individual tax rates. The result is a "double tax" on the same net income. This fact becomes an important consideration when deciding how to sell a corporate business.

A corporation files an income tax return in one of many variants of Form 1120: *U.S. Corporation Income Tax Return*. Corporations come in all sizes and are organized for many purposes. In keeping with the scope of this book, we limit our discussion to the sale of small business corporations. By "small" we mean an entity which has 35 or fewer shareholders, and which was initially capitalized at $10,000,000 (10 million) or less . . . mostly less. Obviously — and intentionally — we are eliminating the corporate goliaths of our day.

There are several ways to sell a small business corporation. Therefore, in this chapter we want to describe the alternatives in some detail. In so doing, we highlight the tax rules that affect the gain or loss consequences to the individual shareholders. After all, these persons are the "owners" of the corporation and are the ones most affected by the tax ramifications of a sale.

It's the Balance Sheet

When selling a corporation, what are you really selling?

You are selling the balance sheet: its assets, liabilities, and stockholders' equity. You are selling the whole ball of wax in one fell swoop. It boils down to the fact that you are selling (or exchanging) stock in the corporate entity. Corporate stock, as we all know, is a *capital asset*. It is not an item that is sold in the ordinary, day-to-day activities of the corporate business.

In the corporation world, a majority of the common stock shareholders have to vote on whether or not to put the business up for sale. Often, a special shareholders' meeting is called for this purpose. The pros and cons of selling are discussed, and a vote is taken: either by voice, ballot, or proxy. It is an up-or-down vote: yea or nay. It is preceded with such specific questions as—

1. Shall the XYZ Corporation be sold?
2. If "Yes," which of the following sales options do you approve?

    (a) ☐ , (b) ☐ , (c) ☐ , (d) ☐

The results of the voting have to be recorded in the Official Minutes of the corporation.

Before the voting issue is raised, all shareholders should have received a copy of the latest balance sheet on the company. This provides the shareholders with a quantitative snapshot of the current net worth of their business. This is its *book value*: not its market value or its asking price at time of sale. Ordinarily, the balance sheet does not show intangibles such as goodwill, customer lists, company know-how, covenants not to compete, etc. Nevertheless, the balance sheet gives each inquiring-minded shareholder a good handle on where the company stands. In the ordinary course of affairs, when dividends are paid out, the balance sheet is not of particular concern to shareholders. It is of great concern when the business is being prepared for sale.

An edited version of a corporate balance sheet, as it appears on page 4 of Form 1120, is presented in Figure 11.1. Many accounting firms use a different arrangement from the format on a federal tax return. We think that, at time of sale, shareholders should insist on getting the *tax format* of a balance sheet rather than an accounting format. The reason is that there are certain disclosures on the tax format which may not be communicated to shareholders otherwise. This withholding of information is most likely in closely-held corporations where five or fewer persons own 50.1% or more of the corporate stock. In these close corporations, there tend to be various self-dealings between the controlling principals and the earnings and profits of the corporation. The tax format of a balance sheet requires the separate listing of such "suspect" items as loans **to** stockholders, investment assets, loans **from** stockholders, long-term liabilities, capital surplus, retained earnings, treasury stock, and so on.

Your Stock's Book Value

Upon receiving a current balance sheet on your corporation, one of the first questions to ask is: How many shares of common stock are outstanding? This information is not on the balance sheet. You might also ask about preferred stock, although in small corporations — of 35 or fewer shareholders — the issuance of preferred stock is rare. Preferred stock has a fixed redemption value without voting power. Common stock, on the other hand, participates in all of the earnings and profits of the business, and has all the voting power.

Once you know how many common shares are outstanding, you can determine the *book value* of your shares from the balance sheet. Knowing the book value, a comparison can be made with what you paid for the shares. This gives you a good idea of whether your company has been well managed or not. A buyer is going to want this information; shouldn't you as a seller also have it?

To establish the book value of your stock, you first compute the net worth of the business from the balance sheet data. This is the total assets at the *end* of the accounting period (target date for the vote or sale) minus the total liabilities. **Caution:** the tax format

Schedule L: Form 1120		BALANCE SHEET		
		End of Tax Year		Beginning of Tax Year	
	Assets				
1	Cash on hand				
2	Accounts receivable				
	Less uncollectables	< >		< >	
3	Inventory on hand				
4	U.S. Gov. obligations				
5	Tax-exempt securities				
6	Other current assets				
7	Loans TO stockholders				
8	Mortgages & real estate loans				
9	Other investments				
10	Buildings and depreciables				
	Less depreciation taken	< >		< >	
11	Depletable assets				
	Less depletion taken	< >		< >	
12	Land (net of 10 &11)				
13	Amortizable intangibles				
	Less amortization taken	< >		< >	
14	All other assets				
	Total Assets ▶				
	Liabilities				
15	Accounts payable				
16	Notes payable (<1 year)				
17	Other current liabilities				
18	Loans FROM stockholders				
19	Notes payable (1 yr or more)				
20	All other liabilities				
	Total Liabilities ▶				
	Stockholders Equity				
21	Capital stock: preferred				
	Plus common stock				
22	Capital surplus (paid-in)				
23	Retained earnings - App.				
24	Retained earnings - Unapp.				
25	Less Treasury stock		< >		< >
	Total Equity ▶				
	TOTAL LIABILITIES & STOCKHOLDERS EQUITY ▶				

Fig. 11.1 - Edited Version of Balance Sheet on Corp. Form 1120

does not show a line for total liabilities alone. The preprinted official line is: "Total liabilities *and stockholder's equity*." One needs to separate these two items. We have done this for you in Figure 11.1 by inserting a subtotal line for total liabilities.

For illustration purposes, assume that there are 9,280 shares outstanding. The initial authorization was for 10,000 shares at $100 par, which means that 720 shares remain as treasury stock. Assume that the company's net worth (assets minus liabilities) is $2,115,290. On these assumptions, the book value per share is

$$\$2,115,290 \div 9,280 \text{ sh} = \$227.94$$

Compared to the initial value of $100 per share, the company appears to have been managed well.

C- versus S-Type Corporations

A small business corporation may operate as one of two tax types. There is a C-type corporation and an S-type corporation. The key difference between the two is the classes of stock issued and the tax treatment of the shareholders.

A C corporation can issue various classes of stock: voting, nonvoting, preferred, common, restricted, registered, etc. There is no statutory limit to the number of shareholders involved. C corporations are expected to pay dividends periodically from their earnings and profits. Before the dividends are distributed, however, the corporation pays income tax on the net earnings and profits for each operating year. When the dividends are distributed, the shareholders pay a "second tax" on the same income. The corporate rates and individual rates are comparable to each other. Thus, there is a true double-tax effect.

In contrast, an S corporation has only one class of stock. It must be all voting common stock. Secondly, the number of shareholders is limited to **not more than** 75 [IRC Sec. 1361(b)(1)(A)]. Furthermore, all shareholders must be individuals, and must be citizens or residents of the U.S. Although the number and type of shareholders are limited, the amount of capitalization is not limited.

There is another, more important, distinguishing feature of an S corporation. Under tax code Sections 1362 and 1363, its shareholders *can elect* to be tax treated as a **partnership** rather than as a corporation. If they so elect, the corporation is not taxed on its net earnings. Instead, the earnings and profits are passed through to the shareholders for taxation at their individual rates. This means that there is no second tax on the same income as in the case of C corporations. An S corporation files Form 1120S: *U.S. Income Tax Return for an S corporation.*

To get favorable S corporation treatment, ALL shareholders must consent to the election. They do this by signing Form 2553: *Election by a Small Business Corporation.* To take effect, the form must be filed within 2-1/2 months after the *beginning* of the corporate year. The form not only requires the name, signature, and Tax ID of each shareholder, it also requires that each shareholder's number of shares be indicated.

In Figure 11.2, we present a summary of the C- versus S-type corporate activities.

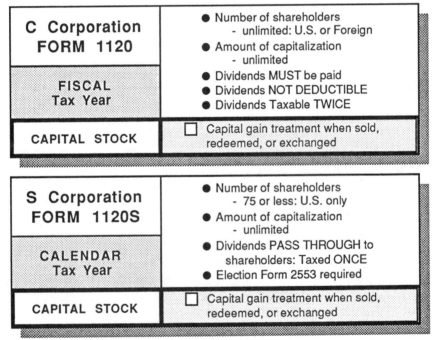

Fig. 11.2 - A Synopsis Comparison of C and S Corporations

The fact that C and S corporations are tax treated differently during ordinary operations raises the question: Are they tax treated differently at the time of the sale of the business?

The answer is "No." Section 1371 makes it clear that, at time of redemptions, liquidations, and reorganizations, the rules applicable to C corporations are also applicable to S corporations. This means that when either a C or S corporation is offered for sale, the shareholders as owners are treated the same. They are selling a business by selling their stock in the corporate entity.

Beware of Securities Laws

When you sell a corporation as a going business, what are you really selling? You are selling stock: called "securities." These securities represent your ownership and title to the assets on, and external to, the balance sheet of the corporate entity. Our use of the pronoun "you" includes all of the stockholders/shareholders of the enterprise.

When you put the business up for sale — either directly or through a broker — you are making a "public offering" thereof. When you make a public offering of securities, there's another federal bureaucracy to contend with. This is the Securities and Exchange Commission (SEC). It, like the IRS, also has tons and tons of regulations. The essence of the SEC regulations is that any public offering of securities must be *registered* as such . . . unless the offering is statutorily exempted. The registration of securities for public offerings is costly, frustrating, and time-consuming. The fees and commissions alone approach 10% of the authorized initial capitalization of the business entity.

Specifically, there are three forms of exemptions from the federal securities laws that are applicable to small corporations for sale. These are: (a) intrastate offerings, (b) private offerings, and (c) small public offerings. The intrastate exemption requires that the entire issue of securities be offered and sold exclusively to residents of the state where the business is incorporated. While this avoids federal laws, it may not avoid state laws on the sale of securities.

The federal exemption for private offerings is limited to accredited investors comprising no more than 35 purchasers. An "accredited investor" is an individual or entity with an average annual income above $200,000 or a net worth exceeding $1,000,000 (1 million). Otherwise, there is no dollar limit to the aggregate offering total sale price.

The exemption for small public offerings requires that the aggregate offering price not exceed $5,000,000 (5 million). This 5 million limit is reduced by the amount of securities sold during the previous 12 months. There is no limit to the number of purchasers involved. However, if the number of purchasers is limited to 35 or fewer, the exemption can be extended to $7.5 million.

None of the above exemptions avoids the offerer's liability for fraud, misrepresentation, or omission of material fact in his "sales pitch." The most famous SEC rule on fraud is **Rule 106-5**. This rule especially applies to the sale or purchase of unregistered securities, including exempt securities and the securities of closely held corporations. These are all classed as *restricted stock*. Rarely does a small business corporation with 35 or fewer shareholders apply for registration of its stock. Therefore, the prudent thing to do is to touch base with state and federal securities regulators when the corporation is being offered for sale in bulk.

Sale-of-Assets Option

If you are totally intimidated by the securities laws, federal or state, there is a simple way out. You sell the corporate assets without selling the corporate stock. That is, you sell the assets as though the entity were a proprietorship instead of a corporation. When the sale formally closes, the stock is redeemed . . . and cancelled. When a corporation redeems and cancels its own stock, there is no selling of securities of any kind. The securities laws do not apply.

Selling assets instead of stock is particularly attractive when there are just a few stockholders or where there are certain liabilities that a buyer doesn't want to take on. Furthermore, there is encouragement in the tax code when a corporation is dissolved or liquidated in exchange for the surrender of all stock by the shareholders.

Directly on point is Section 331: *Gain or Loss to Shareholders in Corporate Liquidations*. Its subsections (a) and (b) read as follows:

(a) Amounts received by a shareholder in a distribution in complete liquidation of a corporation shall be treated as in full payment **in exchange for** *the stock.*

(b) Section 301 (relating to effects on shareholder of distributions of property) shall **not** *apply to any distribution . . . in complete liquidation.* [Emphasis added.]

Subsection 331(a) is saying that if all of the corporate assets are sold and tax accounted for *within* the corporation, and thereafter distributions are made to shareholders "in complete liquidation," the *distributions* are treated as an exchange. The distributions are not taxable to the corporation, because — as an exchange — they are taxable to the shareholders as capital gain or capital loss.

Subsection 331(b) is saying that the distributions of property, dividends, and retained earnings and profits are not characterized as ordinary gain or loss, if they are made within a reasonable time (usually 12 months) after the adoption of a plan of liquidation. This enables the shareholders to accumulate all earnings and profits until the time of liquidation, without paying tax in the interim. They must, however, adopt a *Plan of Liquidation* by a majority of the voting shares. A certified copy of the plan is attached to Form 966: *Corporate Dissolution or Liquidation* and filed with the IRS within 30 days of the majority vote.

As a footnote to the above, Section 331 has to be interpreted in the light of Section 336: *Gain or Loss Recognized on Property Distributed in Complete Liquidation.* It says—

*Gain or loss shall be recognized to a liquidating corporation on the distribution of **property** in complete liquidation as if such property were sold to the distributees at its fair market value.*

Direct Sale of Stock

The sale-of-assets option tends to be a drawn-out affair, especially if there is haggling over the pricing of some of the assets. In contrast, the direct sale of stock is much simpler. All shareholders do not have to agree to selling their stock, but a majority — or 50.1% — must agree. We call the 50.1% holders the *controlling interests* of the corporation. They can make private offerings of their shares to accredited investors . . . wherever.

When an individual buyer, or several such buyers, purchase the controlling stock of a going corporation, they take over the entire operation. This includes the assets, liabilities, cash on hand, accounts receivable, retained earnings, goodwill, and all. They do not have to renegotiate equipment or building leases, employment contracts, supplier contracts, customer lists, and so on. It is as though the former controlling interests stepped aside, and the new owners took their place. It is a simple transfer of stock ownership. It can be either a one-on-one transfer (seller A to purchaser A, etc.)

or a bulk transfer to several buyers who divide their interests up differently from the former interests.

Some 49.9% of the original shareholders can be dead opposed to the sale. Nevertheless, the 50.1% control. Those who remain behind when the new controlling interests take over run the risk of the corporation being plundered of its liquid and more valuable assets. This could materially depress the value of their original shares. With this possibility as a threat over their heads, they are often induced to sell their shares to associates of the acquiring interests at a discount — usually 10% to 20% or so — off of the price paid to the majority shareholders.

In a direct stock sale, the tax accounting for the sale is quite simplified. The broker or accountant handling the stock transfers needs to take only three steps. These are—

1. Make sure that the stock certificates are properly reassigned or transferred by endorsement over to the purchaser or purchasers.
2. Make the proper substitution of names, Tax ID's, etc. in the corporate capital accounts for the shareholders.
3. Prepare Form 1099-B (Proceeds from Broker Transactions) for each selling shareholder, and file with the IRS and the corresponding state tax agency.

Each selling shareholder then tax reports his own gain or loss on Schedule D (Form 1040): Capital Gains and Losses. The process is analogous to, but slightly more cumbersome than, selling publicly traded stock through a financial brokerage firm.

Part Sale, Part Redemption

Sometimes, a small, well-run corporation may have substantial liquid assets or cash that would boost the price the buyer would have to pay for the seller's stock. There are no tax benefits to a buyer when he buys cash or its equivalent from a corporate seller. In these situations, the seller should plan on *redeeming* some of the stock. The objective would be to slim down the cash excess before selling the remaining stock to an outsider.

In other cases, the corporation may own excess assets. These are assets that are unlikely to be wanted by any outside buyer. No buyer wants to pay for something that he doesn't expect to use after closing the sale. If these excess assets have some nostalgic or other continuing-use value to any of the existing shareholders, it is better to distribute such items in the form of stock redemptions. Otherwise, they become a detrimental bargaining element in the negotiations for your best stock price.

When redeeming shares prior to the direct sale of stock to outsiders, there are the *disproportionate redemption* rules to worry about. These rules are addressed in Section 302(b): ***Redemptions Treated as Exchanges***, if certain conditions are met. The two basic conditions are: (1) the 50% rule, and (2) the 80% rule. The purpose of these disproportionate rules is to prevent the distribution of dividends (out of earnings and profits) from being recharacterized as transactional gain or loss on the sale/redemption/exchange of a capital asset.

The 50% rule requires that, after a redemption, or after a series of planned redemptions within one tax year, the redeeming shareholder owns less than 50% of the voting stock of the continuing corporation. In addition, the 80% rule must also be met.

The 80% rule requires that the *holding ratio* of a redeeming shareholder be less than 80% of his pre-redemption holdings. For example, suppose shareholder X owns 40% of the voting stock before redeeming any of his shares. After a partial redemption, he still owns 35% of the stock. His holding ratio after the redemption is 87.5% (35% ÷ 40%). Even though after the redemption he owns less than 50% of the stock, his holding ratio change is not less than 80%. Hence, his redemption would be treated as a dividend, rather than a capital asset exchange. To qualify as a redemption/exchange, his after-redemption holdings must be no more than 31.9% of the voting stock. (80% of the 40% pre-redemption holdings is 32%. Thus, "less than 80%" would be 31.9% or less.)

These disproportionate redemption rules are very important when trying to achieve capital gain treatment for the redemptions, prior to the remaining stock being sold to outsiders. Because of this importance, we depict these concepts in Figure 11.3. The Figure 11.3 rules make sense, once you realize that they are preparatory to selling a corporate business outright.

Deemed Sale: 80% of Stock

A special situation arises when a corporation — *not* an individual — purchases 80% or more of the stock of an offering or target corporation. When this happens, the deemed sale-of-assets rule of Section 338 comes into play. This tax code section is titled:

REDEMPTIONS OF VOTING STOCK		
Rule	**BEFORE**	**AFTER**
1	Any %	Less than 50% of total shares remaining
2	Any %	Less than 80% of BEFORE's holding percentage
E X A M P L E	40% of total shares outstanding	35% of total shares remaining - DISQUALIFIES
		Less than 32% of shares remaining - QUALIFIES
PURPOSE:	To prevent ordinary dividends from being recharacterized as capital gains	

In the EXAMPLE AFTER column, a separate box reads: 40% x 80% equals 32%

Fig. 11.3 - The "Disproportionate Rule" for Partial Redemptions

Certain Stock Purchases Treated as Asset Acquisitions. This is an extremely complicated tax law. The basic law itself consists of about 3,000 words; the "regulations thereunder" consist of over 90,000 words (about 150 pages of fine-print text).

Under Section 338, a corporation making a qualified stock purchase can elect to treat the corporation whose stock is being purchased (target corporation) as having sold all of its assets on the acquisition date at fair market value. A "qualified stock purchase" is the purchase of at least 80% of the total voting power and value of the target corporation during a 12-month acquisition period. When this happens, the target corporation's tax year immediately ends. Its short-year tax return must recognize gain or loss on the *deemed sale* of its assets, even though the target corporation sold only its stock therein. This forces the selling shareholders into an awkward tax position. Unless they act promptly, they can be double taxed on the earnings and profits as dividends **and** as capital gain or loss on the disposition of their (stepped-up basis) share holdings.

Some relief from this double taxation is provided in subsection 338(h)(14): *Coordination with collapsible corporation rules.* If, within one year following the acquisition date, the minority shareholders adopt a plan of liquidation of their own, all of the original shareholders can get capital gain/loss treatment. Otherwise, the target corporation becomes an affiliate of the takeover corporation. The original stockholders are then reissued shares in the conglomerate entity.

Reorganization Exchanges

Shareholders of a small corporation who want to switch stock with another corporation, possibly a publicly traded one, will find Section 354 to be quite advantageous. This section deals with tax-deferred exchanges of stock-for-stock under certain conditions. The conditions require that a *Plan of Reorganization* be adopted by a majority of the shareholders, upon which all assets are transferred to the reorganized entity. The prior business must continue after the reorganization.

Section 354 is titled: ***Exchanges of Stock and Securities in Certain Reorganizations.*** Its general rule, Section 354(a), reads—

*No gain or loss shall be recognized if stock or securities in a corporation a party to a reorganization are, in pursuance of the plan of reorganization, **exchanged solely for stock o r securities** in such corporation or in another corporation a party to the reorganization.* [Emphasis supplied.]

The emphasized phrase is the crux of the matter. The value of the stock or securities surrendered must exact-equal the value of those received. The total number of shares may differ, but their total value before and after the exchange must remain the same. If there is an excess or a shortage on one side of the transaction or the other, the exchange — for tax deferment purposes — is invalid. Otherwise, the ideal arrangement is to enhance the number of shares to the selling shareholders into a more readily salable form for subsequent piecemeal dispositions. This way, each shareholder can sell or not sell his stock, as he sees tax fit.

Section 368 defines seven types of acceptable reorganizations: A, B, C, D, E, F, and G. Type A (*statutory merger*), Type B (*stock-for-stock*), and Type C (*stock-for-assets*) appear to be the more common plans for taking advantage of Section 354.

The IRS regulations are fuzzy as to how to report a reorganization on the "selling" corporation's tax return. Since the corporation continues in existence after the exchange of stock, presumably some highlighted notation should be made directly on the face of Form 1120 (or 1120S). In the upper right-hand white space, enter a notation such as—

Type ___ REORGANIZATION: See Attached

Summary of the Basics

The thrust in this chapter is that the individual taxpayer is selling his ownership interest in a corporate business strictly with the intention of getting capital gain treatment (rather than dividend treatment) on the proceeds therefrom. This occurs only when selling a capital asset. Common stock in a corporation of any size has long been tax recognized as a capital asset. Selling — or redeeming/exchanging — a capital asset means parting with all ownership rights and title to that asset.

The ownership of a corporation is unique in that it can be divided up into many units or shares, each share being a separate capital asset of its own. Consequently, selling a corporation provides choices among many alternatives. These alternatives include selling assets, selling stock, redeeming stock, and exchanging stock.

The ownership of common stock in a corporate entity is a basic form of legal rights known as a security. There are other forms of corporate securities such as preferred stock, warrants, bonds, debentures, and long-term notes. In more formal terms, a "security" is an instrument representing the *unconditional obligation* of a corporation to pay a specified sum of money. Because of random commingling of terms, the phrase "stock or securities" is frequently used when selling a corporation.

In addition to the business risks when selling a corporation, there are certain legal risks. The most intimidating is being labeled as a dealer in securities rather than as a seller of a business. When so labeled, great care is required to avoid allegations of fraud, misrepresentation, or omissions of material fact. One way to divert this labeling is to *legend the stock* as being "unregistered" and therefore "restricted" in its transactional dispositions.

Reducing the Risks

Corporate stock transactions are a breeding ground for litigious activity. Always lurking in the woodwork is the risk of being accused of violating securities laws and engaging in fraudulent activities. There is no guarantee against these dangers — ever. The best one can do is to exercise due diligence, make adequate disclosure, and pursue defensive accounting.

After all, your real objective is to sell your business and extract from the transaction the best tax features that you can. You are offering your business to a limited number of potential buyers who are business knowledgeable. After the sale, the new owner-shareholders will take over and continue the active conduct of the business to make it an even greater success than you did. How can this possibly be interpreted as selling securities to the general public?

Still, the possibility remains. To help reduce this risk, we classify the corporate selling activities into three "price tag" categories. These categories are—

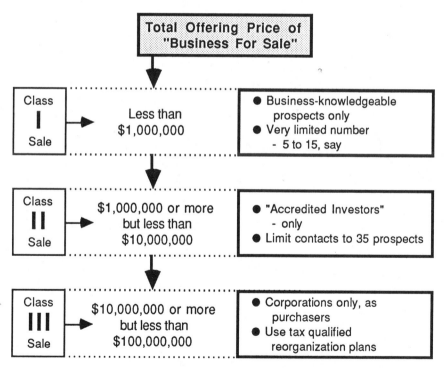

Fig. 11.4 - Reducing the Risk of Being a "Dealer" in Securities

Class I   —   less than $1,000,000 (1 million) in total sale price

Class II   — $1,000,000 or more but less than $10,000,000 (10 million)

Class III   — $10,000,000 or more but less than $100,000,000 (100 million)

A snapshot summary of these classifications (indicating the preferred type of buyers) is presented in Figure 11.4.

A Class I corporation sale often involves a potential buyer consisting of only three to five principals. These are persons who have had some business experience of their own, and who are seeking to expand into a corporate entity from a proprietorship or a partnership. To these few persons, buying into an existing corporation by buying the controlling interests therein makes practical sense. As long as the total number of solicitation contacts is limited, rarely would the onus of securities infractions arise.

A Class II corporation sale should limit all potential buyer contacts to persons who are "accredited investors." These are individuals whose average annual gross income for the past three years is over $200,000 per year, or whose current net worth is over $1,000,000. So long as no more than 35 persons in this category have been contacted, there appears to be a safe harbor securities exemption here.

A Class III corporation sale should focus only on corporations as potential buyers. Preferably, these acquiring corporations would be amenable to participating in a tax recognized reorganization where the assets or stock of the selling corporation are acquired solely in exchange for new stock in the combined entity. Could stock-for-stock in a corporation exchange be heralded as offering securities for sale to the general public? Some surrogates of intimidation might still make the allegation. But it would be entirely moot if the acquiring corporation exchanged its SEC-registered stock for the selling corporation's unregistered stock.

12

POST-SALE MATTERS

It Can Take Up To 3 Years Or More After The Sale Of A Business To Clarify All Tax, Legal, And Regulatory Matters. There Is Some Likelihood Of A Lawsuit, As Well As Need To Renegotiate The Sale Price And Terms. Examination And Scrutiny Of "Final" Tax Returns Of The Business — Federal, State, And Local — Should Be Anticipated. If A Corporation, Formal WINDING DOWN Procedures Are Required By The State Where Incorporated. Multi-Asset Exchange Sales — Believed To Be "Tax Free" — Are Very Complex. The Ideal Is A Section 354 REORGANIZATION, Followed By Piecemeal Sales In The Public Domain.

The signing of a contract for the sale of your business, and the signing of all "closing papers" therewith — including tax returns — does not mean that you are out of the woods. Inevitably, a number of post-sale matters will arise. Some of these matters will be frustrating, some will be pure dogwork, and a few — unfortunately, only a few — will be pleasurable anecdotes of the sales event.

The most successful sale is when the buyer and seller remain on good terms after the sale. But, this does not always happen. Any sale of a business involves much give and take. Mature parties to the sale accept the give-and-take as a process of life. However, there are third parties with peripheral interests that come on the scene afterwards to raise questions about the finality of the transactions. We call these interests: *the sale spoilers.*

Most sale spoilers are attorneys, government agencies, and disgruntled employees — in that order. Attorneys are great flaw-pickers in every written instrument; regulatory and tax agencies are great hind-sighters on what should have been done; disgruntled employees often have had a legitimate beef which was not fully addressed before the business was sold.

In addition, all sale-of-business contracts have contingency and warranty clauses which have to be reviewed and fulfilled. And, there are those awful tax returns that have to be finalized and filed.

In this chapter, therefore, we want to address the more substantive post-sale concerns that may affect you. We certainly want to make some plausible suggestions of ways that might minimize the irritations and adversities that can arise. The winding-down period after a sale can take up to three years or more. Much depends on the complexity of the transactions, and on the good faith and diligence of the parties involved. You cannot let your guard down, even though you think the sale is closed.

Anticipate a Lawsuit

We don't want to be a spoiler, ourselves, but there is always the possibility of a lawsuit following a complex transaction such as the sale of a business. It's the price we all pay for condoning a litigious society. Don't overreact; just be aware that it can happen to you.

Once the buyer takes over full ownership and control of your former business, he may discover things that are not as you presented them to be. They may have been unimportant to you because of your familiarity with them over a period of many years. Yet, seeing them through fresh eyes, the buyer may place a greater importance on them than you felt was warranted.

It could be some accounting item, some customer warranty matter, some equipment operating defect, some inventory shortage, some employee behavior, some misinformed creditor . . . some anything! There is just no way of judging ahead of time what might pop up out of the blue.

Usually, the buyer or his agent will make an innocent-sounding inquiry to you about the item (or items) of his concern. You explain the situation as honestly as you can. It was not important to you initially, and it is not important now — you think.

Time passes, and you hear nothing more.

Then, one day, you get a demand letter from a prestigious legal firm. The letter alleges fraud, misrepresentation, omission of material facts, and breach of contract . . . among other things. The buyer wants to rescind the contract, have you return all monies he paid to you, and wants punitive damages on top of it all. If you don't succumb immediately, a lawsuit will be filed. This is your one and only notice of intent.

You show the letter to your attorney. Before you can work things out amicably with the buyer, you are caught up in a legal quagmire that goes on . . . and on . . . and on. Regardless of the ultimate outcome on the underlying issue(s), you lose — and the buyer loses. In legal wranglings over business issues, only attorneys win.

We are not saying that you will face a lawsuit. Many sales go through with no adverse after-effects. Some do not. All we are saying is that, for some unimaginable reason, a lawsuit can happen. So, just anticipate the possibility.

Review the Warranty Clauses

Every Contract for Sale of a business has contingency and warranty clauses in it. These are not traps planted to catch the unwary. They are prudent precautionary measures because nothing is final (until it is final). There are always some remnants that tend to be ongoing. Such features should be reviewed within 90 days after the sale closing. A 90-day period is adequate for the buyer to begin getting a feel for the business and uncovering items on which he may have questions.

The buyer's main obligations under the contract are to make payments in money or property under the terms specified, and to assume certain debts, liabilities, and covenants that he was made aware of. Your obligations, on the other hand, are to fulfill all of the warranties that you made to him. You have given certain assurances concerning the condition of the business and its assets, the accuracy of financial statements, and disclosures regarding regulatory, tax, legal, or labor matters that are imminent or pending. You should have a natural curiosity about the status of all remnant matters yourself.

After you have reviewed the contract with a clear head, pick up your telephone, call the buyer, and ask if he, too, has had an opportunity to review the instrument. Whether he has or not, suggest that the two of you — or four of you (no attorneys) — get together and review matters that may still be pending. Besides, you'd like to see his operation and see how he is doing. A friendly after-the-sale meeting is a good way to sense if there are any undercurrents of dissatisfaction roaming around. If there are, probe them gently with the sincere intent of being helpful.

After the meeting, take another look at the contract. Look for the paragraph about Arbitration of Disputes. No business contract should be prepared without one. It's there, just above where you and the buyer signed the agreement. Read that paragraph in full. It will start out something like—

All controversies arising under or in connection with, or relating to any alleged breach of this agreement, shall be submitted to a panel of_____ arbitrators. . . . [etc.]

This is your cue that the attorney or attorneys who prepared the contract are at least amenable to arbitration, before barging headlong into a lawsuit. If genuine controversies do develop, give arbitration a chance.

Be Open to Renegotiation

When you and the buyer signed the contract, each of you put your best foot forward trying to get the best price and terms that you could. In the process, each of you may have made commitments that are difficult (post-sale) to fulfill. Or, matters may come up after the fact that were truly and inadvertently unforeseen. Accept these likelihoods as part of the risk of doing business.

Suppose, for example, that a year after the sale closed, the IRS sends a notice to you at your former business address that it wants to "field audit" your business. The audit will cover several years that preceded the sale. Who bears the burden on this matter? You? The buyer? Who?

Most buyers will refuse to be involved in a tax audit that focuses on any period of time prior to the sale closing. Furthermore, some buyers may construe the audit notification as evidence that something wasn't done right in your business. They begin to get leery and suspicious themselves. Their skittishness becomes a problem for you. Little do they realize that the IRS is "winging it" for more revenue only.

When the IRS learns that your business has been sold subsequent to the year(s) selected for audit, it gets panicky over its ability to collect. It thrusts upon you *and* the buyer Form 2045:

Transferee Agreement. This form requires that the transferee (the buyer)—

(1) acknowledge that he has received assets from a transferor (you, the seller),

(2) assume and agree . . . *to pay the amounts of any and all Federal income or profits taxes finally determined or adjudged as due and payable by the transferor,* and

(3) will not resell, retransfer, or reassign any of the assets without prior written amount from the IRS.

Form 2045 must be signed by the transferee. If the transferee/buyer is a corporation, its board of directors must authorize the signing through a resolution of agreement recorded in its corporate minutes.

Can't you sense what will happen when a buyer is IRS confronted with a Form 2045 Transfer Agreement to sign? He's not going to be very friendly to the seller anymore. He's going to want some kind of compensation for his inconvenience and assumption of your tax deficiencies. Most likely, he is going to want to renegotiate the contract in some manner. Be aware of such possibility, and be open minded about it.

Expedite Your Tax Return

A situation like the above happens because of the inertia of the IRS bureaucracy, and the time lag between selling the business and filing the tax returns therewith. The buyer becomes unsettled and begins withholding contingency payments from you.

What do you do to avoid such a situation? We have three specific suggestions that can be helpful.

One. Try to arrange the sale so that its closing takes place within the last three months of your taxable year. This narrows the span of time between the sale closing and the tax return for reporting the sale. If more than three months transpire, details of the sale fade as attention turns to new projects and to new entrepreneurial roles.

Two. Prepare your year-of-sale return promptly and get it filed on time. In fact, get it filed ahead of time! Before the sale closed, you should have had some parallel accounting effort going on with the objective of completing the business portion of your return within 30 days after the sale closes. There is no greater personal satisfaction than having the applicable portion of a tax return completed simultaneously with completing a major business transaction.

Three. This may astound you. But our third suggestion is: Actually request an audit! There is a special form for this purpose. It is Form 4810: *Request for Prompt Assessment.* This is a one-page form on which you list the particular tax return(s) and tax year(s) for which you want expedited IRS attention. It — supposedly — cuts the ordinary 3-year administrative processing time down to 18 months. At least you are doing your part in trying to clear up any remnant matters as expeditiously as possible.

As important, send a copy of Form 4810 to your buyer. By so doing, you are putting him on notice that you are prepared for audit. You are also putting him on notice to stop his skittishness and squeamishness of interpreting an audit as being an adverse reflection on your conduct of business. Form 4810 implies that you are prepared to bite the bullet . . . and move ahead.

The same expeditious effort applies to state and local agencies. There are *final* returns to be filed for income taxes, sales taxes, employment taxes, property taxes; there are licensing, recording, and regulatory bodies to be notified. Do all these things — as summarized in Figure 12.1 — while the excitement of the sale is still fresh in mind.

Winding Down a Corporation

If the business you sold was a corporation, there are special winding down (dissolution) procedures. These are **state** procedures: not federal. All that the IRS requires is that Form 966: *Corporate Dissolution or Liquidation,* be filed *after* the state dissolution procedures have been complied with. All corporations are incorporated under state laws: not federal. The IRS recognizes these state laws. Consequently, it insists that a formal **Certificate of Dissolution** be issued by the incorporating state.

As an owner or co-owner of a corporate business, you cannot walk away from it, like you can with a proprietorship or partnership. A corporation is a creation of law: not of man (like a proprietorship or partnership). It has a birth, a life, and a death.

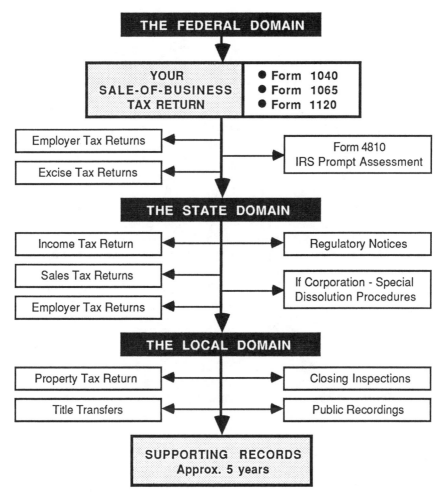

Fig. 12.1 - Post-Sale Cleanup of Tax & Related Matters

After its life ceases, it has an "estate" which has to be dissolved. The dissolution procedures differ from state to state. The Secretary of State in the state of incorporation has to be contacted for the required legal forms.

Let us use the state of California for illustration purposes. California requires that the Certificate of Dissolution be issued by the Secretary of State, Corporate Division, Legal Review Branch. Before issuance, the winding down procedures are:

1. Call a shareholders' final meeting and adopt a resolution to dissolve.
2. The resolution is to be verified by a copy of the official minutes (summarizing events from startup to shutdown), signed by the president and secretary of the corporation.
3. Prepare a "Certificate of Election to Wind Up and Dissolve," indicating the number of voting shares and that the majority voted in favor of the dissolution.
4. Request from the Franchise Tax Board a *Tax Clearance Certificate*; attach a copy of the shareholders' election to dissolve.
5. Pay a minimum franchise tax of $800.
6. File a "final" California corporation income tax return, to which is attached a copy of the final federal return.
7. Pay the amount of California tax as computed.
8. Complete and file "Assumption of Tax Liability" forms, in the event that the self-computed tax is understated.
9. When the Tax Clearance Certificate is received, prepare a Certificate of Dissolution which is signed by three members of the Board of Directors.

As the final step, the tax clearance certificate and the directors' certificate of dissolution are forwarded to the Secretary of State. After a reasonable period of time and verification of the associated records, the Secretary of State of California issues a formal, gold-embossed, imprinted seal **Certificate of Dissolution**. The concluding words on this document are:

IN WITNESS WHEREOF, I execute this certificate and affix the Great Seal of the State of California this _____ (date) _____ .

/s/ _____
                 Secretary of State

Attach a photocopy of the gold-embossed dissolution certificate to Federal **Form 4810** (Prompt Assessment) when requesting prompt attention to your corporation's final returns (Form 1120 or Form 1120S). Also attach a photocopy to IRS Form 966: *Corporate Dissolution or Liquidation*. These forms convey your bona fide desire to wrap up your business-sold affairs expeditiously. Unfortunately, you won't get much cooperation from the IRS on this.

Form 8594 Revisited

Whether a corporation or not, and whether or not a prompt assessment is requested, whenever a business is sold there are certain attachments to the final return that **will be** IRS reviewed. One of these is Form 8594: Asset Acquisition Statement. (Recall Chapter 7 for refresher purposes.) There is opportunity with the form to "juggle matters" by one or more of the *10-percent owners* in the entity sold. A "10-percent owner" is—

Any person who holds 10 percent or more (by value) of the interests in such entity immediately before the transfer. [IRC Sec. 1060(e)(2)(A).]

Why does the IRS target these owner persons?

Answer: Because of their temptation to shift personal service income from themselves to one or more intangible assets that have been sold.

Personal service income is subject to *four* separate taxes, namely: (1) ordinary income tax, (2) alternative minimum tax, (3) social security tax, and (4) medicare tax. In contrast, an intangible such as a covenant not to compete is subject to treatment as a capital asset, where only *one* (preferential) tax rate applies. You have to admit that there is a close functional analogy between personal service matters and covenant-not-to-compete matters. Personal service income is never allowable as an inclusive amount in the total sale price of a business.

If the IRS disallows a portion of the total sale price as personal service income, the sale price is reduced. All of the property allocations therewith have to be redetermined.

For example, suppose the entity sold was a partnership of three members, each of whom was a 10-percent owner. The total sale price was $500,000, of which $100,000 was allocated to a 3-year covenant not to compete. By hocus-pocus and waving its magic wand, suppose the IRS "determined" that the fair market value of the covenant was $40,000. It would then arbitrarily assert that the $60,000 difference was personal service income (allocable at $20,000 to each of the three partners). The total sale price, therefore, for Form 8594 purposes would be $440,000. This means that all tangible and intangible assets of the sale would have to be reallocated. Instead of the previous allocation amount of $500,000, the redetermined allocable amount would be $440,000.

All subordinate allocations of property would have to be redetermined proportionately.

The redetermining of prior seller-buyer allocations is what Part III: *Supplemental Statement*, of Form 8594 is all about. Part III of Form 8594 is where the IRS increases or decreases the transferred property allocations relative to those previously reported. This is the reverse whipsaw problem depicted back in Figure 7.3. The IRS loves to whipsaw you at every chance it can.

Part III of Form 8594 also can be used for amending a return after sale, where the total consideration paid has been increased or decreased by the parties themselves. The most common alterations in consideration would result from—

(a) voluntary renegotiation of the sale price,
(b) recommended arbitration settlement, or
(c) court-ordered changes following the conclusion of a lawsuit (initiated by either party).

Form 6252: Installment Sale

When a small business is sold in proprietorship or partnership form, the most common arrangement for payment terms is via an installment note. There are cash payments over an extended period of time, at a stated rate of interest. When this arrangement occurs, Form 6252: *Installment Sale Income*, is a required attachment to a return. Here, the term "income" refers to payments on principal only. Consequently, care is required to separate the principal portion of a payment from its interest portion. The interest portion does **not** go on Form 6252. (The interest goes on Schedule B, Form 1040.) Form 6252 is required for the year of sale, and for every year thereafter in which you receive a payment — in money, property, debt relief, or pledge loan — towards the installment obligation.

In Figure 12.2, we present an overview of the format and contents of Form 6252. In said figure, we stress the "mechanics" of the form, rather than the precise line numbers and entry captions on the official version of it. The form applies only when there is an overall gain (or gross profit) from the sale.

To illustrate the computational mechanics of Form 6252, let's return to the installment note in Chapter 9: Sale of Proprietorship. For the Schedule C sale, there was a $125,000 installment note specifically earmarked for three intangibles, namely: copyright,

Form 6252	INSTALLMENT SALE INCOME	Year

Use Separate Form for Each Sale

● Description of Property ● Date Acquired ● Date Sold

Part I Gross Profit and Contract Price

          ● Selling Price ➥

> Computational Steps
> & Instructions

          ● Gross Profit ➥

          ● Contract Price ➥

Part II Installment Sale Income

          ● Gross Profit Ratio ➥

> Computational Steps
> & Instructions

          ● Taxable Part ➥

Part III Related Party Installment Sale

Series of Questions and Checkboxes

> Computational Steps
> & Instructions | "second disposition"

Fig. 12.2 - General Format and Contents of Form 6252

customer list, and goodwill. Assuming a $25,000 payment on principal, the computational mechanics on Form 6252 go as follows:

1. Gross sale price (3 intangibles) $125,000
2. Cost or other basis of items sold   -0-
3. Commissions and other expenses of sale   15,000
   [$125,000 x 12%]
4. Add lines 2 and 3   15,000
5. Subtract line 4 from line 1: Gross Profit   110,000

x. **Gross profit ratio**: divide line 5 by line 1   0.8800
y. Payments received during the year   25,000
z. Installment sale income: multiply line y
   by line x. Enter on Form 4797   22,000

The intangible assets covered by the installment note were not on the entity's books at time of the sale. They were created by the sale and, thus, were "held" less than one year. For this reason, the $22,000 amount would go onto Part II (ordinary gains) of Form 4797. Had, say, $35,000 of the $125,000 note been for assets held more than one year, the $22,000 amount would have to be allocated between Part I (capital gains) and Part II. In such case, the respective allocated amounts would be:

$$\text{Part I} \quad (4797): \$22,000 \times \frac{35}{125} = 6,160$$

$$\text{Part II} \quad (4797): 22,000 \times \frac{90}{125} = \underline{15,840}$$

$$\$22,000$$

What the IRS Looks For

What does the IRS look for when it examines Form 6252 after a sale? Right off, it is going to examine the *selling price*. This is the very first dollar-entry on the form. Beyond this entry, there are other special rules under IRC Section 453: Installment Method (of Accounting).

If you sell just one asset only, the selling price entered on Form 6252 presents no major entanglement problem. But when you sell a "bundle of assets," as you do when selling a proprietorship or partnership, you run smack into various allocation problems. In addition, there are special rules regarding personal service income, depreciation recapture income, understatement of interest, and related party transactions. Installment sales often are used by wheelers and dealers to filter and disguise the true tax characteristics of various elements of the sales transaction.

The IRS position is that you could have buried some personal service income in the installment note, in order to avoid self-employment tax. Installment sales cannot be used for deferring personal service income, nor for payments on accounts receivable, nor for merchandise or inventory sold in the ordinary course of trade or business, nor for other items which are noncapital/nonproperty in nature. After all, the purpose of the installment sale method of Form

6252 is to compute the *capital gains portion* of payments on principal received during each tax deferred year.

In three places on the face of the form, an instruction says—

Do not include interest whether stated or unstated.

The purpose of this instruction is to alert you to the imputed interest rules of Section 453A(b)(1) when the sale price exceeds $150,000. These rules are based on Applicable Federal Rates (AFR) published quarterly. If the installment note is for less than 110% AFR, the shortfall becomes *imputed income* on which you pay full tax.

In two places on Form 6252 you are instructed to show "recapture income" from Form 4797. In particular, Section 453(i) says that—

Any recapture income shall be recognized [in full] *in the year of disposition, and any gain in excess of the recapture income shall be taken into account under the installment method.*

What this means is that you could well pay tax on amounts which you have not actually received in the year of sale. When you do this, you increase the basis in the property sold, so that you do not pay a second tax when the recapture amount is actually received.

If you sold your business to one or more family members or close business associates (called: *related persons*), a special rule — subsection 453(e) — comes into play. The essence of this rule is that if a related person within two years after the date of the first disposition resells the business (or any portion of it)—

. . . the amount realized with respect to such second disposition shall be treated as received . . . by the person making the first disposition.

In other words, you can't soften your tax burden by selling to a family member or business friend at lower than fair market value. Form 6252 alerts you to this rule by requiring a ☐ Yes ☐ No answer to the question: *Did the related party resell or dispose of the property ("second disposition")?* If "Yes," you then select among five other checkboxes, and complete eight additional computational steps.

Form 8824 Exchanges

If attached to your return as a consequence of the sale of your business, Form 8824: *Like-Kind Exchanges*, is also subject to the IRS's examination scrutiny. The reason for the scrutiny is that a like-kind exchange experiences no immediate tax. The transaction is *tax deferred*. To get the deferment benefit, the IRS wants to make sure that you understand what *like-kind* means.

Form 8824 is predicated upon Section 1031 of the tax code. This section is titled: Exchange of Property Held for Productive Use or Investment. It is subtitled: *Nonrecognition of Gain or Loss from Exchanges Solely in Kind.* The subsection (a) is very popular among small business owners. Whether a proprietorship, partnership, or corporation, sellers and buyers just love to switch properties around in so-called "tax free exchanges." It is the titular word "Nonrecognition" that is misconstrued as being synonymous with "tax free." Enthusiasts completely overlook the titular words: **from Exchanges Solely in Kind**.

So important is Section 1031(a) that we should quote in full its paragraph (1). This paragraph reads:

(1) In General — No gain or loss shall be recognized on the exchange of property held for productive use in a trade or business, or for investment, if such property is exchanged solely for property of like kind which is to be held either for productive use in a trade or business or for investment. [Emphasis added.]

Since Section 1031 and Form 8824 hinge on "solely for property of like kind," what does like kind mean?

The term "like kind" means properties that have the same character or nature, but are not necessarily of the same grade or quality. The distinction is purely one of class and character only; physical size, shape, color, grade, or quality are irrelevant. For example, real property and personal property are not of the same class. Farmland and nonfarm real estate are of the same class. But livestock of different sexes are not like kind, nor are business-use vehicles and pleasure vehicles. Real estate in the U.S. is not like kind with real estate in a foreign country. A copyright on a novel and a copyright on a song are not like kind, nor is the goodwill of one business like kind with the goodwill of another business. There are subtleties between like and nonlike properties which make for tax interpretation disputes. Cash and nonlike property are fully taxed at the time of the exchange.

Purpose(s) of Form 8824?

Form 8824 is poorly designed and formatted in terms of its computational logic and completeness. Foremost in this regard is that it does not provide for *equity balancing* between the like-kind properties being exchanged. Equity balancing is the first step for determining the extent of nonlike property — or "boot" — that makes the exchange work financially. Missing this procedural inroad, we have to ask the question: What is the real purpose of Form 8824?

This is not a frivolous question. Obtain a copy of the official form (and its instructions) and you'll see what we mean. Fully one-third of page 1 of the form pertains to related person exchanges (as in Form 6252). If there is no exchange with a related party, you are instructed to skip said portion.

Otherwise, the purpose of Form 8824 appears to be three-fold. One purpose is to separate the like-kind properties from the nonlike properties. The second purpose is to tax recognize immediately the gain or loss on nonlike property given up. The third purpose is to establish a *transfer basis* in the like-kind property received.

Purpose 1 is self-evident from the lead-off questions which ask for detailed descriptions of—

1. *Like-kind propety given up*
2. *Like-kind property received*

and the respective dates therewith. All other balancing aspects of the exchange — cash, boot, securities, debt swaps, new loans, etc. — are treated as money received for any nonlike property given up.

Purpose 2 is to compute the gain or loss on the nonlike property given up, and then "tax recognize" it. There is no tax deferment on the nonlike properties involved. This is quite clear from the preprinted instructions on the form which read:

If you gave up property that was not like-kind . . . report the gain or loss . . . as if the exchange had been a sale.

Purpose 3 is to establish the acquisition tax basis in the like-kind property received. Since no gain or loss is recognized when like properties are exchanged, there is a **transfer of basis** involved. This is so that when the exchange-acquired property is later sold, the deferred gain or loss is tax recognized at that time.

Let us illustrate in simple terms what we mean by "Transfer of basis." In our Chapter 9 scenario of a Schedule F sale/exchange, assume that the adjusted basis (cost less depreciation) in the farm animals (1 stallion and 3 brood mares) is $50,000. Even though the properietor acquired 10 acres of farm land worth $135,000, her tax basis in that land is $50,000 . . . plus. The "plus" is the addition of exchange expenses, which in our case would be $16,200 ($135,000 x 12% expense of sale). Hence, the seller's tax basis would start at $66,200 (50,000 + 16,200). It could be more than, or less than, this amount depending on how much "debt swapping" took place between the exchangers.

Exchange computations are extremely complicated. Even for the simplest exact-alike for exact-alike exchange, there are some 40 computational steps. If there are multi-asset exchanges, as there would be when selling a business, the computational steps are multiplied. Yet, Form 8824 shows only 14 steps total . . . for everything!

For example, one of the computational entries on Form 8824 calls for—

Cash received, FMV of other property received, plus net liabilities assumed by other party, reduced (but not below zero) by any exchange expenses you incurred. See instructions.

The instructions tell you to make your own computations on an attachment, and enter the results on the line indicated. All of which means that, computationally, Form 8824 is meaningless.

The Ideal Exchange: Sec. 354

A multi-asset exchange under the rules of Section 1031 is very complicated. So complicated that we do not recommend a Section 1031 exchange when selling a successful business. Instead, we highly recommend a Section 354 exchange. We consider this the ideal selling arrangement for a business with a net worth over $1,000,000 (1 million).

The reason for the $1,000,000 threshold is that the exchange must start as a corporate entity. Only corporations can participate in a Section 354 exchange. Even then, there must be a mutually

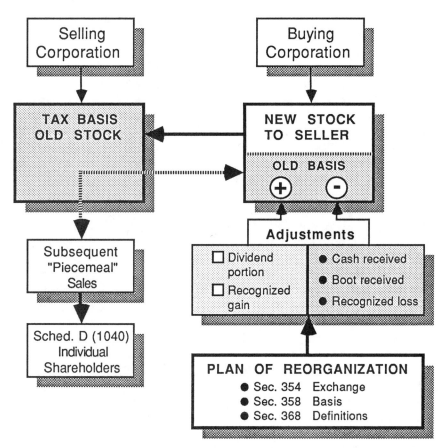

Fig. 12.3 - "Basis Transfer" in Stock-for-Stock Reorganization

acceptable **Plan of Reorganization** between the two entities. Rarely does a buying corporation whose stock is publicly traded, or soon may be, want to engage in exchange negotiations with a selling entity whose total assets are less than $1,000,000. It would rather buy the individual assets.

For refresher purposes, we repeat Section 354(a)(1) that we previously cited in Chapter 11 (on page 11-13). It reads—

*No gain or loss shall be recognized if stock or securities in a corporation a party to a reorganization are, in pursuance of the plan of reorganization, **exchanged solely for** stock or* *securities in such corporation or in another corporation a party to the reorganization.* [Emphasis added.]

The phrase "exchanged solely for" has the same like-kind characteristics of Section 1031. That is, common stock for common stock, preferred stock for preferred stock, and so on. But *not* common stock for preferred stock. Why? Because they are not of the same class. Common stock has voting power, whereas preferred stock does not. Whether the common stock is restricted or registered is immaterial. Such distinction is a gradation or quality issue: not a class issue. Once the conditions for "like class" are met, the transaction becomes essentially a single-asset exchange.

The word "solely" has been interpreted to mean: *substantially all*. This, in turn, has been interpreted to mean that more than 80% of the selling/conveying corporation's stock has been exchanged for equivalent-value stock in the buying/acquiring corporation. This leaves a little slack for cash and "odds and ends" (or boot) to defray the legal and accounting expenses involved. The amount of cash and boot — called: *recognition property* — affects the tax basis of the new stock acquired by the selling corporation.

Once the Section 354 exchange has been made, the tax basis in the new stock of the selling corporation is determined by the rules of Section 358: **Basis to Distributees.** Essentially, this is the old basis in the stock, plus or minus certain adjustments for the exchange expenses and the nonrecognition property. Computationally, these matters are "all taken care of" in the Plan of Reorganization. Nevertheless, we present the gist of this to you in Figure 12.3.

There are two reasons why we characterize a Section 354 as ideal. One, there are no directly applicable preprinted tax forms involved. Secondly, the new stock can be subsequently sold piecemeal in the public trading domain. At such time, the only tax reporting is Form 1099-B (Proceeds of Broker Transactions) and Schedule D (Form 1040): **Capital Gains and Losses.** This is the neatest way of selling a business, once it attains a market value and niche that are attractive to an aspiring corporation . . . which wants to be your buyer.

ABOUT

THE AUTHOR

Holmes F. Crouch

Born on a small farm in southern Maryland, Holmes was graduated from the U.S. Coast Guard Academy with a Bachelor's Degree in Marine Engineering. While serving on active duty, he wrote many technical articles on maritime matters. After attaining the rank of Lieutenant Commander, he resigned to pursue a career as a nuclear engineer.

Continuing his education, he earned a Master's Degree in Nuclear Engineering from the University of California. He also authored two books on nuclear propulsion. As a result of the tax write-offs associated with writing these books, the IRS audited his returns. The IRS's handling of the audit procedure so annoyed Holmes that he undertook to become as knowledgeable as possible regarding tax procedures. He became a licensed private Tax Practitioner by passing an examination administered by the IRS. Having attained this credential, he started his own tax preparation and counseling business in 1972.

In the early years of his tax practice, he was a regular talk-show guest on San Francisco's KGO Radio responding to hundreds of phone-in tax questions from listeners. He was a much sought-after guest speaker at many business seminars and taxpayer meetings. He also provided counseling on special tax problems, such as divorce matters, property exchanges, timber harvesting, mining ventures, animal breeding, independent contractors, selling businesses, and offices-at-home. Over the past 25 years, he has prepared nearly 10,000 tax returns for individuals, estates, trusts, and small businesses (in partnership and corporate form).

During the tax season of January through April, he prepares returns in a unique manner. During a single meeting, he completes the return . . . *on the spot!* The client leaves with his return signed, sealed, and in a stamped envelope. His unique approach to preparing returns and his personal interest in his clients' tax affairs have honed his professional proficiency. His expertise extends through itemized deductions, computer-matching of income sources, capital gains and losses, business expenses and cost of goods, residential rental expenses, limited and general partnership activities, closely-held corporations, to family farms and ranches.

He remembers spending 12 straight hours completing a doctor's complex return. The next year, the doctor, having moved away, utilized a large accounting firm to prepare his return. Their accountant was so impressed by the manner in which the prior return was prepared that he recommended the doctor travel the 500 miles each year to have Holmes continue doing it.

He recalls preparing a return for an unemployed welder, for which he charged no fee. Two years later the welder came back and had his return prepared. He paid the regular fee . . . and then added a $300 tip.

During the off season, he represents clients at IRS audits and appeals. In one case a shoe salesman's audit was scheduled to last three hours. However, after examining Holmes' documentation it was concluded in 15 minutes with "no change" to his return. In another instance he went to an audit of a custom jeweler that the IRS dragged out for more than six hours. But, supported by Holmes' documentation, the client's return was accepted by the IRS with "no change."

Then there was the audit of a language translator that lasted two full days. The auditor scrutinized more than $1.25 million in gross receipts, all direct costs, and operating expenses. Even though all expensed items were documented and verified, the auditor decided that more than $23,000 of expenses ought to be listed as capital items for depreciation instead. If this had been enforced it would have resulted in a significant additional amount of tax. Holmes strongly disagreed and after many hours explanation got the amount reduced by more than 60% on behalf of his client.

He has dealt extensively with gift, death and trust tax returns. These preparations have involved him in the tax aspects of wills, estate planning, trustee duties, probate, marital and charitable bequests, gift and death exemptions, and property titling.

Although not an attorney, he prepares Petitions to the U.S. Tax Court for clients. He details the IRS errors and taxpayer facts by citing pertinent sections of tax law and regulations. In a recent case involving an attorney's ex-spouse, the IRS asserted a tax deficiency of $155,000. On behalf of his client, he petitioned the Tax Court and within six months the IRS conceded the case.

Over the years, Holmes has observed that the IRS is not the industrious, impartial, and competent federal agency that its official public imaging would have us believe.

He found that, at times, under the slightest pretext, the IRS has interpreted against a taxpayer in order to assess maximum penalties, and may even delay pending matters so as to increase interest due on additional taxes. He has confronted the IRS in his own behalf on five separate occasions, going before the U.S. Claims Court, U.S. District Court, and U.S. Tax Court. These were court actions that tested specific sections of the Internal Revenue Code which he found ambiguous, inequitable, and abusively interpreted by the IRS.

Disturbed by the conduct of the IRS and by the general lack of tax knowledge by most individuals, he began an innovative series of taxpayer-oriented Federal tax guides. To fulfill this need, he undertook the writing of a series of guidebooks that provide in-depth knowledge on one tax subject at a time. He focuses on subjects that plague taxpayers all throughout the year. Hence, his formulation of the "Allyear" Tax Guide series.

The author is indebted to his wife, Irma Jean, and daughter, Barbara MacRae, for the word processing and computer graphics that turn his experiences into the reality of these publications. Holmes welcomes comments, questions, and suggestions from his readers. He can be contacted in California at (408) 867-2628, or by writing to the publisher's address.

ALLYEAR Tax Guides
by Holmes F. Crouch

All of the above available at bookstores, libraries, and on the internet